S H O A H

An Oral History of the Holocaust

CLAUDE LANZMANN

The Complete Text of the Film

Preface by Simone de Beauvoir

PANTHEON BOOKS, NEW YORK

English subtitles of the film by A. Whitelaw and W. Byron

Library of Congress Cataloging-in-Publication Data

Lanzmann, Claude.
  Shoah
  Transcription of English subtitles to 1985 French film Shoah.
  1. Holocaust, Jewish (1939-1945)—Drama. 2. Jews—Poland—Drama. I. Shoah (Motion picture) II. Title.
DS135.P6L284 1985   940.53'15'03924   85-16760
ISBN 0-394-74329-6 (pbk.)

Manufactured in the United States of America

BOOK DESIGN BY GUENET ABRAHAM

First Paperback Edition

Shoah is not an easy film to talk about. There is a magic in this film that defies explanation. After the war we read masses of accounts of the ghettos and the extermination camps, and we were devastated. But when, today, we see Claude Lanzmann's extraordinary film, we realize we have understood nothing. In spite of everything we knew, the ghastly experience remained remote from us. Now, for the first time, we live it in our minds, hearts and flesh. It becomes our experience.

Neither fiction nor documentary, *Shoah* succeeds in recreating the past with an amazing economy of means—places, voices, faces. The greatness of Claude Lanzmann's art is in making places speak, in reviving them through voices and, over and above words, conveying the unspeakable through people's expressions.

Places. The Nazis' great concern was to obliterate all traces. But they could not wipe out all the memories, and Lanzmann has succeeded in ferreting out the horrible realities hidden beneath camouflage, like young forests and fresh grass. In ditches on that green field trucks dumped bodies of Jews who had died of asphyxiation during the journey. Into that pretty little stream were thrown the ashes of incinerated corpses. Here are peaceful farms where Polish farmers could hear and even see what was happening in the camps. Here are villages with fine old houses from which the entire Jewish population has been deported.

Claude Lanzmann shows us the Treblinka, Auschwitz and Sobibor railway stations. He walks up the now grass-covered ramps, down which thousands of victims were herded into the gas chamber. I found one of the most heartrending sequences a heap of suitcases, some unpretentious, others more expensive, but all carrying name and address tags. Mothers had carefully packed into them milk powder, talc, baby food. Others had packed clothes, food, medicines. But no one ever had any need of them.

Voices. During most of the film all the voices tell of the same things: the trains that arrived, the wagons being opened and corpses tumbling out, the thirst, the unawareness riddled with fear, the stripping and "disinfection" procedures, the gas chambers being opened. But never does it seem repetitive.

First, because of the different voices. There is the cold, objective—with a few emotional tremors at the beginning—voice of Franz Suchomel, the SS Unterscharführer at Treblinka. It is he who gives the most precise and detailed account of the extermination of each consignment. There are the slightly flustered voices of some Poles—the driver of the locomotive, whom the Germans sustained with shots of vodka, but who could not stand the cries of thirsty children; the Sobibor stationmaster, worried by the sudden silence that had fallen over the nearby camp.

But often the peasants' voices are indifferent or even a little mocking. And then there are the voices of the very rare Jewish survivors of the camps. Two or three have managed to master a seeming serenity. But many can hardly speak—their voices break down and they burst into tears. The fact that many times they speak about the same events does not tire you. To the contrary. You think of the intentional repetition of a musical phrase or leitmotiv. For, with its moments of intense horror, peaceful landscapes, laments and resting places, what *Shoah*'s subtle construction calls to mind is a musical composition. And the whole work is punctuated by the almost intolerable din of trains rushing toward the camps.

Faces. They often say much more than words. The Polish peasants express compassion. But most of them seem indifferent, ironic and even satisfied. The faces of the Jews match what they say. The oddest are the German faces. Franz Suchomel's remains impassive, except when he sings a song glorifying Treblinka and then his eyes light up. But the embarrassed, foxy expressions of the others give the lie to their protestations that they did not know and are innocent.

One of Claude Lanzmann's great skills has in fact been to tell us the story of the Holocaust from its victims' viewpoint, as well as from that of the "technicians" who made it possible but reject all responsibility for it. One of the most typical is the bureaucrat who organized the transport. He explains that special trains were made available to holiday or excursion groups at half-fare. He does not deny that the trains sent to the camps were also special trains, but claims he did not know that the camps meant extermination. He says he assumed they were work camps where the weakest died. His embarrassed, evasive expression belies his claim that he did not know. A little later the historian Raul Hilberg tells us that the Jews who were "resettled" were regarded as vacationers by the travel agency and that the Jews, unwittingly, themselves financed their own deportation, since the Gestapo paid for it with the goods it had confiscated.

Another striking example of how an expression gives the lie to words is given by a German "administrator" of the Warsaw ghetto. He wanted to help the ghetto survive, he declares, to protect it from typhus. But when Claude Lanzmann questions him, he mumbles an answer, his expression becomes distorted, his eyes turn shifty and he is totally confused.

Claude Lanzmann's construction does not follow a chronological order. I should say it is a poetical construction, if I may use the word in connection with such a subject. The Warsaw ghetto, for instance, is described only right at the end of the film, when we already know the remorseless fate of its walled-in inhabitants.

Here again the narrative is not univocal: it is a funeral cantata for several skillfully interwoven voices. Karski, at the time the courier of the Polish government in exile, yielding to the entreaties of two highly placed Jewish leaders, visits the ghetto to report back to the world on what he has seen (to no purpose, moreover). He sees only the ghastly inhumanity of the dying ghetto. The rare survivors of the uprising, crushed by German bombs, speak on the other hand of the efforts made to preserve the humanity of the doomed community. The great historian Hilberg has a long discussion with Lanzmann about the suicide of Czerniakow, who thought he could help the Jews in the ghetto but lost all hope the day of the first deportations.

In my view the end of the film is wonderful. One of the very few survivors of the ghetto uprising stands alone among its ruins. He says he experienced a kind of tranquillity as he thought, "I'm the last of the Jews and I'm waiting for the Germans." And the film immediately cuts to a train hurrying another consignment to the camps.

Like all who have seen the film, I mingle past and present. I have said that the miraculous side of *Shoah* lies in this mingling. I should add that I would never have imagined such a combination of beauty and horror. True, the one does not help to conceal the other. It is not a question of aestheticism: rather, it highlights the horror with such inventiveness and austerity that we know we are watching a great oeuvre. A sheer masterpiece.

Simone de Beauvoir

Here is the complete text—words and subtitles—of my film *Shoah*. The languages that I did not understand, such as Polish, Hebrew, and Yiddish, were translated into French in the body of the film itself (and then translated into English for the American edition). The interpreters—Barbara Janicka, Francine Kaufmann, Madame Apfelbaum—are themselves present on the screen. I have completely respected their method of translation and have included in the text the exact words, the hesitations, the repetitions—all the crutches of the spoken language. Nor have I purged my own questions. When, on the other hand, the people being questioned and I were able to speak in German, without the intervention of a translator, our dialogue was subtitled for the spectators of the film, and these are those subtitles, established by me with Odette Haudebeau-Cadier and Irith Leker, for the French translation you will be reading here.

The subtitling of the film has determined the way in which this book reads: the subtitles reflect very closely the spoken words, but they never express the entirety of what is said. The number of spaces allotted to each subtitle can vary considerably, according to whether the speaker is quiet or passionate, talking fast or slowly. Yet the amount of time in which the spectator can read a subtitle never changes. The faces of those who are speaking, their mimicry, their gestures, in other words, the image itself is the natural support of the subtitle, its incarnation, for the subtitle ideally must not precede or follow the spoken word but coincide exactly with it, flashing at the very instant the word is uttered. The best subtitle, therefore, must at the same time satisfy both those who, having a perfect knowledge of the foreign language involved, could do without it, and those who, able to grasp only a few of the words, are nonetheless given the illusion that they have understood everything. In other words, the subtitle becomes, as it were, invisible. On the screen the subtitle appears and disappears barely born, followed immediately by another one which lives in the same way its short life. Each of these flashes under our gaze, goes back to nothingness as soon as it appears, and it is the number of spaces allowed both by the time of reading and by the shift from one shot to another that determines the length of the sentence, the final cut, frequently violent, because it is the uninterrupted cascade of words that brutally pronounces the death of the subtitle.

On the screen, therefore, subtitles are unessential. Bringing them together, on the other hand, in this book, engraving on page after page the succession of sheer instances that in the film maintain the rhythm imposed by their sequence, having them pass from the inessential to the essential, suddenly gives them another status, another dignity, as it were, a seal of eternity. They have to exist by themselves, to justify themselves without any indication of what is happening, without any image, without any face, without any of the countryside, without a tear, without a silence, without the nine and a half hours of film that constitute *Shoah*.

Incredulous, I read and reread this naked and bloodless text. A strange force seems to have filled it through and through, it resists, it lives its own life. It is the writing of disaster, and that for me is another mystery.

Claude Lanzmann

I will give them an everlasting name.

Isaiah 56:5

The story begins in the present at Chelmno, on the Narew River, in Poland. Fifty miles northwest of Lodz, in the heart of a region that once had a large Jewish population, Chelmno was the place in Poland where Jews were first exterminated by gas. Extermination began on December 7, 1941. At Chelmno four hundred thousand Jews were murdered in two separate periods: December 1941 to Spring 1943 and June 1944 to January 1945. But the way in which death was administered remained the same throughout: the gas vans. Of the four hundred thousand men, women and children who went there, only two came out alive: Michael Podchlebnik and Simon Srebnik. Srebnik, survivor of the last period, was a boy of thirteen when he was sent to Chelmno. His father had been killed before his eyes in the ghetto in Lodz; his mother died in a gas van at Chelmno. The SS placed him in one of the "Jewish work details," assigned to maintaining the extermination camps and slated in turn for death.

With his ankles in chains, like all his companions, the boy shuffled through the village of Chelmno each day. That he was kept alive longer than the others he owed to his extreme agility, which made him the winner of jumping contests and speed races that the SS organized for their chained prisoners. And also to his melodious voice: several times a week, when the rabbits kept in hutches by the SS needed fodder, young Srebnik rowed up the Narew, under guard, in a flat-bottomed boat, to the alfalfa fields at the edge of the village. He sang Polish folk tunes, and in return the guard taught him Prussian military songs. Everyone in Chelmno knew him: the Polish farm folk and German civilians as well, since this Polish province was annexed to the Reich after the fall of Warsaw, germanized and renamed Wartheland. Chelmno was changed to Kulmhof, Lodz to Litzmannstadt, Kolo to Warthbrücken, etc. German colonists had settled everywhere in Wartheland, and there was even a German grade school in Chelmno itself.

During the night of January 18, 1945, two days before Soviet troops arrived, the Nazis killed all the remaining Jews in the "work details" with a bullet in the head. Simon Srebnik was among those executed. But the bullet missed his vital brain centers. When he came to, he crawled into a pigsty. A Polish farmer found him there. The boy was treated and healed by a Soviet Army doctor. A few months later Simon left for Tel Aviv along with other survivors of the death camps.

I found him in Israel and persuaded that one-time boy singer to return with me to Chelmno. He was then forty-seven years old.

"A little white house
lingers in my memory.
Of that little white house
I dream each night."

CHELMNO

Villagers

He was thirteen and a half years old. He had a lovely singing voice, and we heard him.

"A little white house
lingers in my memory.
Of that little white house
I dream each night."

When I heard him again, my heart beat faster, because what happened here . . . was a murder. I really relived what happened.

Simon Srebnik

It's hard to recognize, but it was here. They burned people here. A lot of people were burned here. Yes, this is the place. No one ever left here again.

5

The gas vans came in here. . . . There were two huge ovens, and afterward the bodies were thrown into these ovens, and the flames reached to the sky. It was terrible. No one can describe it. No one can recreate what happened here. Impossible? And no one can understand it. Even I, here, now. . . . I can't believe I'm here. No, I just can't believe it. It was always this peaceful here. Always. When they burned two thousand people—Jews—every day, it was just as peaceful. No one shouted. Everyone went about his work. It was silent. Peaceful. Just as it is now.

> "You, girl, don't you cry,
>   don't be so sad,
>   for the dear summer is nearing . . .
>   and I'll return with it.
>   A mug of red wine, a slice of roast,
>   that's what the girls give their soldiers.
>   When the soldiers march along,
>   the girls open their doors and windows."

Villagers

They thought the Germans made him sing on the river. He was a toy to amuse them. He had to do it. He sang, but his heart wept.

Do their *hearts weep, thinking about that now?*

Certainly, very much so. They still talk about it around

6

the family table. It was public, so everyone knew of it.

He said that was true German irony: people were being killed, and he had to sing. That's what I thought.

Michael Podchlebnik (Israel), the other survivor

What died in him in Chelmno?

Everything died. But he's only human, and he wants to live. So he must forget. He thanks God for what remains, and that he can forget. And let's not talk about that.

Does he think it's good to talk about it?

For me it's not good.

Then why is he talking about it?

Because you're insisting on it. He was sent books on Eichmann's trial. He was a witness, and he didn't even read them. At the time, he felt as if he were dead, because he never thought he'd survive, but . . . he's alive.

Why does he smile all the time?

What do you want him to do, cry? Sometimes you smile, sometimes you cry. And if you're alive, it's better to smile.

S O B I B O R

Hanna Zaïdel (Israel), daughter of Motke Zaïdel, survivor of Vilna (Lithuania)

Why was she so curious about this story?

It's a long story. As a child, I had little contact with my father. He went out to work and I didn't see much of him. Besides, he was a silent man, he didn't talk to me. And when I grew up and was strong enough to face him, I questioned him. I never stopped questioning him, until I got at the scraps of truth he couldn't tell me. It came out haltingly. I had to tear the details out of him, and finally, when Mr. Lanzmann came, I heard the whole story for the second time.

Motke Zaïdel and Itzhak Dugin, survivors of Vilna

But the Lithuanian forests are denser than the Israeli forests, no?

The place resembles Ponari: the forest, the ditches. It's as if the

8

bodies had been burned here. Except there were no stones in Ponari.

Of course, the trees are similar, but taller and fuller in Lithuania.

Jan Piwonski

Is there still hunting here in the Sobibor forest?

Yes, there are lots of animals of all kinds.

Was there hunting then?

Only manhunts. Some victims tried to escape. But they didn't know the area. At times people heard explosions in the minefield, sometimes they'd find a deer, and sometimes a poor Jew who tried to escape.

That's the charm of our forests: silence and beauty. But it wasn't always so silent here. There was a time when it was full of screams and gunshots, of dogs' barking, and that period especially is engraved on the minds of the people who lived here then. After the revolt the Germans decided to liquidate the camp, and early in the winter of 1943 they planted pines that were three or four years old, to camouflage all the traces.

That screen of trees? That's where the mass graves were?

Yes. When he first came here in 1944, you couldn't guess what had happened here, that these trees hid the secret of a death camp.

CHELMNO

Michael Podchlebnik

How did he react, the first time he unloaded corpses, when the gas van doors were opened?

What could he do? He cried. The third day he saw his wife and children. He placed his wife in the grave and asked to be killed. The Germans said he was strong enough to work, that he wouldn't be killed yet.

Was the weather very cold?

It was in the winter of 1942, in early January. The bodies weren't burned, they were buried, and each row was covered with dirt. They weren't being burned yet. There were around four or five layers. The ditches were funnel-shaped. They dumped the bodies in these ditches, and they had to lay them out like herrings, head to foot.

S O B I B O R

Motke Zaïdl and Itzhak Dugin

So it was they who dug up and burned all the Jews of Vilna?

Yes. In early January 1944 we began digging up the bodies.

When the last mass grave was opened, I recognized my whole family. Mom and my sisters. Three sisters with their kids. They were all in there. They'd been in the earth four months, and it was winter. They were very well preserved. I recognized their faces, their clothes too.

They'd been killed relatively recently?

Yes.

And it was the last grave?

Yes.

The Nazi plan was for them to open the graves, starting with the oldest?

Yes. The last graves were the newest, and we started with the oldest, those of the first ghetto. In the first grave there were twenty-four thousand bodies.

The deeper you dug, the flatter the bodies were. Each was almost a flat slab. When you tried to grasp a body, it crumbled, it was impossible to pick up. We had to open the graves, but without tools. They said: "Get used to working with your hands."

With just their hands!

When we first opened the graves, we couldn't help it, we all burst out sobbing. But the Germans almost beat us to death. We had to work at a killing pace for two days, beaten all the time, and with no tools. The Germans even forbade us to use the words "corpse" or "victim." The dead were blocks of wood, shit, with absolutely no importance. Anyone who said "corpse" or "victim" was beaten. The Germans made us refer to the bodies as *Figuren,* that is, as puppets, as dolls, or as *Schmattes,* which means "rags."

Were they told at the start how many Figuren *there were in all the graves?*

The head of the Vilna Gestapo told us: "There are ninety thousand people lying there, and absolutely no trace must be left of them."

TREBLINKA

Richard Glazar (Switzerland), survivor

It was at the end of November 1942. They chased us away from our work and back to our barracks. Suddenly, from the part of the camp called the death camp, flames shot up. Very high. In a flash, the whole countryside, the whole camp, seemed ablaze. It was already dark. We went into our barracks and ate. And from the window, we kept on watching the fantastic backdrop of flames of every imaginable color: red, yellow, green, purple. And suddenly one of us stood up. We knew . . . he'd been an opera singer in Warsaw. His name was Salve, and facing that curtain of fire, he began chanting a song I didn't know:

> "My God, my God,
> why hast Thou forsaken us?
>
> We have been thrust into the fire before,
> but we have never denied Thy Holy Law."

He sang in Yiddish, while behind him blazed the pyres on which they had begun then, in November 1942, to burn the bodies in Treblinka. That was the first time it happened. We knew that night that the dead would no longer be buried, they'd be burned.

S O B I B O R

Motke Zaïdl and Itzhak Dugin

When things were ready, they poured on fuel, and touched off the fire. They waited for a high wind. The pyres usually burned for seven or eight days.

||||||||||||||||||||||||||||||||||||||||||||||||||||||||||||||||||||||||||||||||||||||||||||||||||||||||||||||||||||||

C H E L M N O

Simon Srebnik

There was a concrete platform some distance away, and the bones that hadn't burned, the big bones of the feet, for example, we took. There was a chest with two handles. We carried the bones there, where others had to crush them. It was very fine, that powdered bone. Then it was put into sacks, and when there were enough sacks, we went to a bridge on the Narew River, and dumped the powder. The current carried it off. It drifted downstream.

||||||||||||||||||||||||||||||||||||||||||||||||||||||||||||||||||||||||||||||||||||||||||||||||||||||||||||||||||||||

A U S C H W I T Z

Paula Biren (Cincinnati), survivor

You never returned to Poland since?

I wanted to, many times, but what would I see? How can I face it? My grandparents are buried in Lodz, and at one point I

heard from somebody that visited Poland that they wanted to level off the cemetery, do away with the cemetery. How can I return to visit then?

When did your grandparents die?

My grandparents? My grandparents died in the ghetto, quickly. They were elderly, and within a year my grandfather died, and my grandmother the next year, in the ghetto.

Mrs. Pietyra (present-day Auschwitz)

Mrs. Pietyra, you live in Auschwitz?

Yes, I was born here.

And you've never left Auschwitz?

No, never.

Were there Jews in Auschwitz before the war?

They made up eighty percent of the population. They even had a synagogue here.

Just one?

Just one, I think.

Does it still exist?

No, it was wrecked. There's something else there now.

Was there a Jewish cemetery in Auschwitz?

It still exists. It's closed now.

Closed? What does that mean?

They don't bury there now.

||||||||||||||||||||||||||||||||||||||||||||||||||||||||||||||||||||||||||||||||||||||||||||||||||||||||||||||||||||||||||||||||||||||||||||||||||||||||||||||||

W L O D A W A

Mr. Filipowicz (present-day Wlodawa)

Was there a synagogue in Wlodawa?

Yes, and it's very beautiful. When Poland was ruled by the czars, that synagogue already existed. It's even older than the Catholic Church. It's no longer used. There's no one to go to it.

These buildings haven't changed?

Not at all. There were barrels of herrings here, and the Jews sold fish. There were stalls, small shops, Jewish business, as the gentleman says. That's Barenholz's house. He sold wood. Lipschitz's store was there. He sold cloth. This was Lichtenstein's.

What was there, opposite?

A food store.

A Jewish store?

Yes. There was a notions shop here—it sold thread, needles, odds and ends; and there were also three barbers.

Was that fine house Jewish?

It's Jewish.

And this small one?

Also.

And the one behind it?

These were all Jewish.

This one on the left too?

That one too.

Who lived in it? Borenstein?

Borenstein, yes. He was in the cement business. He was very handsome, and cultivated. Here there was a blacksmith named Tepper. It was a Jewish house. A shoemaker lived here.

What was his name?

Yankel.

You get the feeling Wlodawa was entirely a Jewish city.

Yes, because it's true. The Poles lived farther out; the center was wholly Jewish.

||||||||||||||||||||||||||||||||||||||||||||||||||||||||||||||||||||||||||||||||||||||||||||||||||||||||||||||||||||||||||||||||||||||||||||||||||||||||||||||||||||||||

A U S C H W I T Z

Mrs. Pietyra

What happened to the Jews of Auschwitz?

They were expelled and resettled, but I don't know where.

What year was that?

It began in 1940, which was when I moved here. This apartment also belonged to Jews.

According to our information, the Auschwitz Jews were "resettled," as they say, nearby, in Benzin and Sosnowiec, in Upper Silesia.

Yes, because those were Jewish towns.

Does she know what happened to the Jews of Auschwitz?

I think they all ended up in the camp.

That is, they returned to Auschwitz?

Yes. All kinds of people from everywhere were sent here. All the Jews came here . . . to die.

‖‖

W L O D A W A

Mr. Filipowicz

What'd they think when Wlodawa's Jews were all deported to Sobibor?

What could we think? That it was the end of them, but they had foreseen that.

How so?

Even before the war, when you talked to the Jews, they foresaw their doom, he doesn't know how. Even before the war they had a premonition.

21

How were they taken to Sobibor? On foot?

It was frightful. He watched it himself. They were herded on foot to a station called Orkrobek. There they put the old people first into waiting cattle cars, then the younger Jews, and finally the kids. That was the worst: they threw them on top of the others.

K O L O

Mr. Falborski (present-day Kolo)

Were there a lot of Jews in Kolo?

A great many. More Jews than Poles.

And what happened to the Kolo Jews? Was he an eyewitness?

Yes. It was frightful. Frightful to see. Even the Germans hid; they couldn't look. When the Jews were herded to the station, they were beaten; some were even killed. A cart followed the convoy to pick up the corpses.

Those who couldn't walk, the slain?

Yes, those who'd fallen.

Where did this happen?

The Jews were collected in the Kolo Synagogue. Then they were herded to the station, where the narrow-gauge railroad went to Chelmno.

It happened to all the Jews in the area, not just in Kolo?

Absolutely. Everywhere. Jews were also murdered in the forests near Kalisz, not far from here.

||||||||||||||||||||||||||||||||||||||||||||||||||||||||||||||||||||||||||||||||||||||||||||||||||||||||||||||||||||||||||||||||||||||||||||||||||||||||||||||||||||||

T R E B L I N K A

Abraham Bomba (Tel Aviv), survivor

There was a sign, a small sign, on the station of Treblinka. I don't know if we were at the station or if we didn't go up to the station. On the line over there where we stayed there was a sign, a very small sign, which said "Treblinka." The first time in my life I heard that name "Treblinka." Nobody knew. It was not a place. There was not a city. There is not even a small village. Jewish people always dreamed, and that was part of their life, part of their messianic hope, that some day they're going to be free. That dream was mostly true in the ghetto. Every day, every single night, I dreamed about that. I think that's going to be good. Not only the dream but the hope conserved in a dream.

The first transport from Czestochowa was sent away on the day after Yom Kippur. The day before Succoth, there was a second transport . . . I was together with them. I know in my heart that something is not good, because if they take children, if they take old people, they send them away, that means it is not good. What they said is they take them away to a place where they will be working. But on the other hand, an old woman, a little child of four weeks or five years, what is work? It was a foolish thing, but still, we had no choice—we believed in them.

Czeslaw Borowi (present-day Treblinka)

He was born here in 1923, and has been here ever since.

He lived at this very spot?

Right here.

Then he had a front-row seat for what happened?

Naturally. You could go up close or watch from a distance. They had land on the far side of the station, To work it, he had to cross the track, so he could see everything.

Does he remember the first convoy of Jews from Warsaw on July 22, 1942?

He recalls the first convoy very well, and when all those Jews were brought here, people wondered, "What's to be done with them?" Clearly, they'd be killed, but no one yet knew how. When people began to understand what was happening, they were appalled, and they commented privately that since the world began, no one had ever murdered so many people that way.

While all this was happening before their eyes, normal life went on? They worked their fields?

Certainly they worked, but not as willingly as usual. They had to work, but when they saw all this, they thought: "Our house may be surrounded. We may be arrested too!"

Were they afraid for the Jews too?

Well, he says, it's this way: if I cut my finger, it doesn't hurt him. They knew about the Jews: the convoys came in here, and then went to the camp, and the people vanished.

Villagers (present-day Treblinka)

He had a field under a hundred yards from the camp. He also worked during the German occupation.

He worked his field?

Yes. He saw how they were asphyxiated; he heard them scream; he saw that. There's a small hill; he could see quite a bit.

What did this one say?

They couldn't stop and watch. It was forbidden. The Ukrainians shot at them.

But they could work a field a hundred yards from the camp?

They could. So occasionally he could steal a glance if the Ukrainians weren't looking.

He worked with his eyes lowered?

Yes.

He worked by the barbed wire and heard awful screams.

His field was there?

Yes, right up close. It wasn't forbidden to work there.

So he worked, he farmed there?

Yes. Where the camp is now was partly his field. It was off limits, but they heard everything.

It didn't bother him to work so near those screams?

At first it was unbearable. Then you got used to it.

You get used to anything?

Yes.

Now he thinks it was impossible. Yet it was true.

Czeslaw Borowi

So he saw the convoys arriving. There were sixty to eighty cars in each convoy, and there were two locomotives that took the convoys into the camp, taking twenty cars at a time.

And the cars came back empty?

Yes. Here's how it happened: the locomotive picked up twenty cars and took them to the camp. That took maybe an hour, and the empty cars came back here. Then the next twenty cars were taken, and meanwhile, the people in the first twenty were already dead.

Railway workers (present-day Treblinka)

They waited, they wept, they asked for water, they died. Sometimes they were naked in the cars, up to 170 people. This is where they gave the Jews water, he says.

Where was that?

Here. When the trains came, they gave the Jews water.

Who gave the Jews water?

We did, the Poles. There was a tiny well, we took a bottle and . . .

Wasn't it dangerous to give them water?

Very dangerous. You could be killed for giving a glass of water. But we gave them water anyway.

Villager

Is it very cold here in winter?

It depends. It can get to minus fifteen, minus twenty.

Which was harder on the Jews, summer or winter? Waiting here, I mean.

He thinks winter, because they were very cold. They were so packed in the cars, maybe they weren't cold. In summer they suffocated; it was very hot. The Jews were very thirsty. They tried to get out.

Were there corpses in the cars on arrival?

Obviously. They were so packed in that even those still alive sat on corpses for lack of space.

Didn't people here who went by the trains look through the cracks in the cars?

Yes, they could look in sometimes as they went by. Sometimes when it was allowed, we gave them water too.

How did the Jews try to get out? The doors weren't opened. How'd they get out?

Through the windows. They removed the barbed wire and came out of the windows. They jumped, of course. Sometimes they just deliberately got out, sat down on the ground, and the guards came and shot them in the head.

Railway workers

They jumped from the cars. What a sight! Jumping from the windows. There was a mother and child.

A Jewish mother?

Yes. She tried to run away, and they shot her in the heart. Shot the mother. This gentleman has lived here a long time; he can't forget it.

Villager

He says that now he can't understand how a man can do that to another human being. It's inconceivable, beyond understanding.

Once when the Jews asked for water, a Ukrainian went by and forbade giving any. The Jewish woman who had asked for water threw her pot at his head. The Ukrainian moved back, maybe ten yards, and opened fire on the car. Blood and brains were all over the place.

Czeslaw Borowi

Lots of people opened the doors, or escaped through the windows. Sometimes the Ukrainians fired through the car walls. It happened chiefly at night. When the Jews talked to each other, as he showed us, the Ukrainians wanted things quiet, and they asked . . . yes, asked them to shut up. So the Jews shut up and the guard moved off. Then the Jews started talking again, in their language, as he says: *ra-ra-ra,* and so on.

What's he mean, la-la-la? *What's he trying to imitate?*

Their language.

No, ask him. Was the Jews' noise something special?

They spoke Jew.

Does Mr. Borowi understand "Jew"?

No.

Abraham Bomba

We were in the wagon; the wagon was rolling in the direction east. A funny thing happened, like maybe it's not nice to say, but I will say it. Most of the people, not only the majority, but ninety-nine percent of the Polish people when they saw the train going through—we looked really like animals in that wagon, just our eyes looked outside—they were laughing, they had a joy, because they took the Jewish people away. What was going on in the wagon, the pushing and the screaming: "Where is my child?" and "Where is my this?" and "A little bit of water." And people were not only starving, they were choking—it was hot. It was just Jewish luck. In September, at that time when it is usually raining, it is usually cool, it was hot like hell. We had nothing inside. For a child like mine, about the age of three weeks, there was not a little drop of water. Not only not water for the mother, but not for anybody else.

Henrik Gawkowski (Malkinia)

Did he hear screams behind his locomotive?

Obviously, since the locomotive was next to the cars. They screamed, asked for water. The screams from the cars closest to the locomotive could be heard very well.

Can one get used to that?

No. It was extremely distressing to him. He knew the people behind him were human, like him. The Germans gave him and the other workers vodka to drink. Without drinking, they couldn't have done it. There was a bonus—that they were paid not in money, but in liquor. Those who worked on other trains didn't get this bonus. He drank every drop he got because without liquor he couldn't stand the stench when he got here. They even bought more liquor on their own, to get drunk on.

Abraham Bomba

We arrived in the morning about, I would say, six, six-thirty. On the other side of the tracks, more trains standing there. And I was watching through about eighteen, twenty, maybe more, wagons going away. And after about an hour or so the wagons coming back without the people. My train stayed there until about twelve o'clock.

〰〰〰〰〰〰〰〰 ——————————

Henrik Gawkowski

From the station to the unloading ramp in the camp is how many miles?

Four.

Abraham Bomba

We stayed there at that station waiting to go into Treblinka. Some of the German SS came around and were asking us what we have. So we said some of the people have gold, they have diamonds, but we want water. So they said: "Good, give us the diamonds, we bring you water." They took the diamonds away; they didn't bring any water at all.

How long did the trip last?

The trip lasted from Czestochowa to Treblinka about twenty-four hours with interruption, waiting at Warsaw and also waiting at Treblinka to go into Treblinka camp. At the last train we went in over there, but like I mentioned before, I saw many trains coming back but the trains were without the people. So I said to myself: "What happened to the people? We don't see any people, just trains coming back."

33

Richard Glazar

We traveled for two days. On the morning of the second day we saw that we had left Czechoslovakia and were heading east. It wasn't the SS guarding us, but the Schutzpolizei, the police, in green uniforms. We were in ordinary passenger cars. All the seats were filled. You couldn't choose. They were all numbered and assigned. In my compartment there was an elderly couple. I still remember: the good man was always hungry and his wife scolded him, saying they'd have no food left for the future.

Then, on the second day, I saw a sign for Malkinia. We went on a little farther. Then, very slowly, the train turned off of the main track and rolled at a walking pace through a wood. While he looked out—we'd been able to open a window—the old man in our compartment saw a boy . . . cows were grazing . . . and he asked the boy in signs, "Where are we?" And the kid made a funny gesture. This: (draws finger across his throat).

A Pole?

A Pole. It was where the train had stopped. On one side was the wood, and on the other were fields. We saw cows watched over by a young man, a farmhand.

And one of you questioned him?

Not in words, but in signs, we asked: "What's going on here?" And he made that gesture. Like this. We didn't really pay much attention to him. We couldn't figure out what he meant.

Villagers

Once there were foreign Jews—they were this fat—riding in passenger cars. There was a dining car, they could drink, and walk around too. They said they were going to a factory. On arrival they saw what kind of a factory it was.

We'd gesture that they'd be killed.

These people made that sign?

He says the Jews didn't believe it.

But what does that gesture mean?

That death awaited them.

Czeslaw Borowi

The people who had a chance to get near the Jews did that to warn them that they'd be hanged, killed, slain. Even foreign Jews from Belgium, Czechoslovakia, from France too, surely, and from Holland and elsewhere. These didn't know, but the Polish Jews knew. In the small cities in the area, it was talked about. So the Polish Jews knew, but the others didn't.

Who'd they warn, Polish Jews or the others?

All the Jews. He says the foreign Jews came in passenger cars,

they were well dressed, in white shirts, there were flowers in
the cars, and they played cards.

Henrik Gawkowski

*From what I know, that was very rare, Jews shipped in passenger
cars. Most arrived in cattle cars.*

It's not true.

It's not true? What did Mrs. Gawkowska say?

She said he may not have seen everything. He says he did.
Once, at the Malkinia station, for example, a foreign Jew left
the train to buy something at the bar. The train pulled out and
he ran after it, to catch up to it.

Czeslaw Borowi

*So he went past these "Pullmans," as he calls them, containing those
Jews who were calm, unsuspecting, and he made that gesture to
them.*

To all the Jews, in principle.

He just went along the platform! Ask him!

Yes. The road was as it is now. When the guard wasn't looking, he made that gesture.

Henrik Gawkowski

Ask Mr. Gawkowski why he looks so sad.

Because I saw men marching to their death. Not far—a mile and a half from here. That's where the rail line into the camp was.

Did Mr. Gawkowski—aside from the trains of deportees—he drove from Warsaw or Bialystok to the Treblinka station—did he

ever drive the deportee cars into the camp from the Treblinka station?

Two or three times a week for around a year and a half.

That is, throughout the camp's existence?

Yes. This is the ramp.

Here he is, he goes to the end with his locomotive, and he has the twenty cars behind him.

No, they're in front of him. He pushed them.

||||||||||||||||||||||||||||||||||||||||||||||||||||||||||||||||||||||||||||||||||||||||||||||||||||||||||||||||||||||||||||||||||||||||||||||||||||||||||||||||||||

S O B I B O R

Jan Piwonski (Sobibor Station)

In February 1942 I began working here as an assistant switch-man.

The station building, the rails, the platforms are just as they were in 1942? Nothing's changed?

Nothing.

Exactly where did the camp begin?

If we go there, I'll show you exactly. Here there was a fence that ran to those trees you see there. And another fence that ran to those trees over there.

So I'm standing inside the camp perimeter, right?

That's right.

Where I am now is fifty feet from the station, and I'm already outside the camp. This is the Polish part, and over there was death.

Yes. On German orders, Polish railmen split up the trains. So the locomotive took twenty cars, and headed toward Chelmno. When it reached a switch, it pushed the cars into the camp on the other track we see there. Unlike Treblinka, the station here is part of the camp. And at this point we are inside the camp.

Where we are now is what was called the ramp, right?

Yes, those to be exterminated were unloaded here.

So where we're standing is where 250,000 Jews were unloaded before being gassed?

Yes.

Did foreign Jews arrive here in passenger cars too?

Not always. Often the richest Jews, from Belgium, Holland, France, arrived in passenger cars, sometimes even in first class. They were usually better treated by the guards. Especially the convoys of Western European Jews waiting their turn here. Polish railmen saw the women making up, combing their hair, wholly unaware of what awaited them minutes later. They dolled up. And the Poles couldn't tell them anything: the guards forbade contact with the future victims.

I suppose there were fine days like today.

Unfortunately, some were even finer.

A U S C H W I T Z

Rudolf Vrba (New York), survivor

There was a place called the ramp where the trains with the Jews were coming in. They were coming in day and night, and sometimes one per day and sometimes five per day, from all sorts of places in the world. I worked there from August 18, 1942, to June 7, 1943. I saw those transports rolling one after another, and I have seen at least two hundred of them in this position. I have seen it so many times that it became a routine. Constantly, people from the heart of Europe were disappearing and they were arriving to the same place with the same ignorance of the fate of the previous transport. And the people in this mass . . . I knew of course that within a couple of hours after they arrived there, ninety percent would be gassed or something like that. I knew that. Somehow in my thinking it was difficult for me to comprehend that people can disappear in this way. Nothing is going to happen, and then there

comes the next transport, and they don't know anything about what happened to the previous transport, and this is going on for months, on and on.

So what happened was the following. Say a transport of Jews was announced to come at two o'clock. When the transport arrived at the station of Auschwitz, an announcement came to the SS. Now one SS man came and woke us up and we moved to the ramp. We immediately got an escort and were escorted to the ramp—say we were about two hundred men. And lights went on. There was a ramp, around the ramp were lights, and under those lights were a cordon of SS. There was one every ten yards with gun in hand. So we were in the middle and were waiting for the train, waiting for the next order.

Now when all this was done—everybody was there—the transport was rolled in. This means in a very slow fashion the locomotive, which was always in the front, was coming to the ramp, and that was the end of the railway line, that was the end of the line for everybody who was on the train. And now the train stopped and the gangster elite marched on the ramp, and in front of every second or every third wagon, and sometimes in front of every wagon, one of those *Unterscharführers* was standing with a key and opened the locks, because the wagons were locked.

Now inside there were people, of course, and you could see the people looking through the windows because they didn't know what was happening. They had many stops on the journey—some of them were ten days on the journey, some were two days on the journey—and they didn't know what this particular stop means. The door was opened and the first order they were given was *"Alle heraus"*: "Everybody out." And in order to make it quite clear, they usually started with those walking sticks to hit the first or second or third. They were like sardines in those cars. If they expected on that day four or five or six transports, the pressure of getting out from the wagons was high. Then they used sticks, clubs, cursing, etcetera. Sometimes, if it was good weather, the SS used to deal with it differently. I mean I was not surprised if they were in a different mood and exhibited a lot of humor, like saying "Good morning, madame" and "Will you walk out, please." Oh yes, oh yes. And "How nice that you arrived. We are so sorry that it wasn't too convenient, but now things will become different."

||||||||||||||||||||||||||||||||||||||||||||||||||||||||||||||||||||||||||||||||||||||||||||||||||||||||||||||||||||||||||||||||||||||||||||||||||||||||||||||||||||||||||||

T R E B L I N K A

Abraham Bomba

When we came into Treblinka, we didn't know who the people were. Some of them had red armbands, some of them blue: Jewish commandos. Falling out from the train, pushing out each other, over there losing each other, and the crying and the hollering. And coming out, we started one to the right, one to the left, the women to the left and men on the right. And we had no time even to look at each other because they start hitting us over the head with all kinds of things and it is very, very painful. You didn't know what had happened, you had no time to think. All you heard was the crying and all you heard all the time was the hollering of the people.

||||||||||||||||||||||||||||||||| ————————————

Richard Glazar

And suddenly it started: the yelling and screaming. "All out, everybody out!" All those shouts, the uproar, the tumult! "Out! Get out! Leave the baggage!" We got out stepping on each other. We saw men wearing blue armbands. Some carried whips. We saw some SS men. Green uniforms, black uniforms. . . .

We were a mass, and the mass swept us along. It was irresistible. It had to move to another place. I saw the others undressing. And I heard: "Get undressed! You're to be disinfected!" As I waited, already naked, I noticed the SS men separating out some people. These were told to get dressed. A passing SS man suddenly stopped in front of me, looked me over, and said: "Yes, you too, quick, join the others, get dressed. You're going to work here, and if you're good, you can be a kapo—a squad leader."

Abraham Bomba

At my transport I was waiting already naked. A man came over and said: "You, you, you, step out." And we stepped out, and they took us a little bit on the side. Some of the people from the transport had an idea what was going on, and they know already that they will not stay alive. Pushing the people—they didn't want to go or they knew already where they go— toward this big door. The crying and the hollering and the shouting that was going on over there! It was impossible. The hollering and the crying was in your ears and your mind for days and days, and at night the same thing. From the howling you couldn't even sleep a couple of nights. All at once at one time everything stopped by a command. It was all quiet. The place where the people went in and just like a command, like everything was dead. Then they told us to make clean the whole place. There were about two thousand people who had

undressed on the outside, to take the whole thing away and to clear up the place. And this has to be done in minutes. Some of the Germans, some of the other people that were there, the Ukrainians and other ones, they start shouting and hitting us that we should do it faster, to carry the bundles to the main place where there were big piles of clothes, of shoes, of other things. And in no time this was as clean as though people had never been on that place. There was no trace, none at all, like a magic thing, everything disappeared.

A U S C H W I T Z

Rudolf Vrba

Whenever a new transport came, the ramp was cleaned absolutely to zero point. No trace from the previous transport was allowed to remain. Not one trace.

||||||||||||||||||||||||||||||||||||||||||||||||||||||||||||||||||||||||||||||||||||||||||||||||||||||||||||||||||||||||||||||||||||||||||||||||||||||||||||||||||||||||||||||||||||

T R E B L I N K A

Richard Glazar

We were taken to a barracks. The whole place stank. Piled about five feet high in a jumbled mass, were all the things people could conceivably have brought. Clothes, suitcases, everything stacked in a solid mass. On top of it, jumping around like demons, people were making bundles and carrying them outside. It was turned over to one of these men. His armband said "Squad Leader." He shouted, and I understood that I was also to pick up clothing, bundle it, and take it somewhere. As I worked, I asked him: "What's going on? Where are the ones who stripped?" And he replied: "Dead! All dead!"

But it still hadn't sunk in, I didn't believe it. He'd used the Yiddish word. It was the first time I'd heard Yiddish spoken. He didn't say it very loud, and I saw he had tears in his eyes. Suddenly, he started shouting, and raised his whip. Out of the corner of my eye I saw an SS man coming. And I understood that I was to ask no more questions, but just to rush outside with the package.

Abraham Bomba

At that time we started working in that place they called Treblinka. Still I couldn't believe what had happened over there on the other side of the gate, where the people went in, everything disappeared, and everything got quiet. But in a minute we find out, when we start to ask the people who worked here before us what had happened to the others, they said: "What do you mean, what happened? Don't you know that? They're all gassed, all killed." It was impossible to say anything—we were just like stones. We couldn't ask what had happened to the wife, to the kid. "What do you mean—wife, kid? Nobody is anymore!" How could they kill, how could they gas so many people at once? But they had a way to do it.

Richard Glazar

All I could think of then was my friend Carel Unger. He'd been at the rear of the train, in a section that had been uncoupled and left outside. I needed someone. Near me. With me. Then I saw him. He was in the second group. He'd been spared too. On the way, somehow, he had learned, he already knew. He looked at me. All he said was: "Richard, my father, mother, brother . . ." He had learned on the way there.

Your meeting with Carel—how long after your arrival did it happen?

It was . . . around twenty minutes after we reached Treblinka. Then I left the barracks and had my first look at the vast space that I soon learned was called "the sorting place." It was buried under mountains of objects of all kinds. Mountains of shoes, of clothes, thirty feet high. I thought about it and said to Carel: "It's a hurricane, a raging sea. We're shipwrecked. And we're still alive. We must do nothing . . . but watch for every new wave, float on it, get ready for the next wave, and ride the wave at all costs. And nothing else."

Abraham Bomba

That's how the day went through, without anything. Not drinking—we went twenty-four hours without water, without anything. We couldn't drink—we couldn't take anything into our mouths, because it was impossible to believe that just a minute, just an hour before, you were part of a family, you were part of a wife or a husband, and now all of a sudden everything is dead.

We went into a special barrack, where I was sleeping right next to the hallway. And over there, that night was the most horrible night for all the people, because of the memory of all those things that people went through with each other—all the joys and the happiness and the births and the weddings and other things—and all of a sudden, in one second, to cut through without anything, and without any guilt of the people, because the people weren't guilty at all. The only guilt they had was that they were Jewish.

Most of us were up all night, trying to talk to each other, which was not allowed. The kapo that was sleeping in the same barrack . . . we were not allowed to talk to each other or to express our views or our minds to each other. And till the morning at five o'clock we start going out from the barrack. In the morning when they had the appeal to go out from the barracks, from our group I would say at least four or five were dead. I don't know how that happened—they must have had with them some kind of poison and poisoned themselves. At least two of them were my close friends. They didn't say anything. We didn't even know they had poison with them.

Richard Glazar

Greenery—sand everywhere else. At night we were put into a barracks. It just had a sand floor. Nothing else. Each of us simply dropped where he stood. Half asleep, I heard some men hang themselves. We didn't react then. It was almost normal.

Just as it was normal that for everyone behind whom the gate of Treblinka closed, there was death, had to be death, for no one was supposed to be left to bear witness. I already knew that, three hours after arriving at Treblinka.

||||||||||||||||||||||||||||||||||||||||||||||||||||||||||||||||||||||||||||||||||||||||||||||||||||||||||||||||||||||||||||||||||

B E R L I N

Inge Deutschkron; born in Berlin and lived there throughout the war (in hiding beginning February 1943); now lives in Israel

This is no longer home, you see. And especially it's no longer home when they start telling me that they didn't know, they didn't know. They say they didn't see. "Yes, there were Jews living in our house, and one day they were no longer there. We didn't know what happened." They couldn't help seeing it. It wasn't a matter of one action. These were actions that were taking place over almost two years. Every fortnight people were thrown out of the houses. How could they escape it? How could they not see it?

I remember the day when they made Berlin *Judenrein*. The people hastened in the streets; no one wanted to be in the streets; you could see the streets were absolutely empty. They didn't want to look, you know. They hastened to buy what they had to buy—they had to buy something for the Sunday, you see. So they went shopping and hastened back into their houses. And I remember this day very vividly because we saw police cars rushing through the streets of Berlin taking people out of the houses. They had herded the Jews together, from factories, from houses, wherever they could find them, and had put them into something that was called "Klu." Klu was a dance restaurant, a very big one. From there they were deported in various transports. They were going off not very far from here on one of the tracks at the Grünewald station, and this was the day when I suddenly felt so utterly alone, left alone, because now I knew we would be one of the very few people left. I didn't know how many more would be underground. This also was the day when I felt very guilty that I didn't go myself and I tried to escape fate that the others could not escape. There was no more warmth around, no more soul akin to us, you understand. And we talked about this. What happened to Elsa? To Hans? And where is he and where is she? My God, what happened to the child? These were our thoughts on that horrible day. And this feeling of being terribly alone and terribly guilty that we did not go with them. Why did we try? What made us do this? To escape fate—that was really our destiny or the destiny of our people.

T R E B L I N K A

Franz Suchomel, SS Unterscharführer

Are you ready?

Yes. We can begin.

How's your heart? Is everything in order?

Oh, my heart—for the moment, it's all right. If I have any pain, I'll tell you. We'll have to break off.

Of course. But your health, in general, is . . .

The weather today suits me fine. The barometric pressure is high; that's good for me.

You look to be in good shape, anyway. Let's begin with Treblinka. I believe you got there in August? Was it August 20 or 24?

The eighteenth.

The eighteenth?

I don't know exactly. Around August 20. I arrived there with seven other men.

From Berlin?

From Berlin.

From Lublin?

From Berlin to Warsaw, from Warsaw to Lublin, from Lublin back to Warsaw and from Warsaw to Treblinka.

What was Treblinka like then?

Treblinka then was operating at full capacity.

Full capacity?

Full capacity! The Warsaw ghetto was being emptied then. Three trains arrived in two days, each with three, four, five thousand people aboard, all from Warsaw. But at the same time, other trains came in from Kielce and other places. So three trains arrived, and since the offensive against Stalingrad was in full swing, the trainloads of Jews were left on a station siding. What's more, the cars were French, made of steel. So that while five thousand Jews arrived in Treblinka, three thousand were dead in the cars. They had slashed their wrists, or just died. The ones we unloaded were half dead and half mad. In the other trains from Kielce and elsewhere, at least half were dead. We stacked them here, here, here and here. Thousands of people piled one on top of another on the ramp. Stacked like wood. In addition, other Jews, still alive, waited there for two days: the small gas chambers could no longer handle the load. They functioned day and night in that period.

Can you please describe, very precisely, your first impression of Treblinka? Very precisely. It's very important.

My first impression of Treblinka, and that of some of the other men, was catastrophic. For we had not been told how and what . . . that people were being killed there. They hadn't told us.

You didn't know?

No!

Incredible!

But true. I didn't want to go. That was proved at my trial. I was told: "Mr. Suchomel, there are big workshops there for tailors and shoemakers, and you'll be guarding them."

But you knew it was a camp?

Yes. We were told: "The Führer ordered a *resettlement program*. It's an *order from the Führer.*" Understand?

Resettlement program.

Resettlement program. No one ever spoke of killing.

I understand. Mr. Suchomel, we're not discussing you, only Treblinka. You are a very important eyewitness, and you can explain what Treblinka was.

But don't use my name.

No, I promised. All right, you've arrived at Treblinka.

So Stadie, the sarge, showed us the camp from end to end. Just as we went by, they were opening the gas-chamber doors, and people fell out like potatoes. Naturally, that horrified and appalled us. We went back and sat down on our suitcases and cried like old women.

Each day one hundred Jews were chosen to drag the corpses to the mass graves. In the evening the Ukrainians drove those Jews into the gas chambers or shot them. Every day!

It was in the hottest days of August. The ground undulated like waves because of the gas.

From the bodies?

Bear in mind, the graves were maybe eighteen, twenty feet deep, all crammed with bodies! A thin layer of sand, and the heat. You see? It was a hell up there.

You saw that?

Yes, just once, the first day. We puked and wept.

You wept?

We wept too, yes. The smell was infernal because gas was constantly escaping. It stank horribly for miles around. You could smell it everywhere. It depended on the wind. The stink was carried on the wind. Understand?

More people kept coming, always more, whom we hadn't the facilities to kill. The brass was in a rush to clean out the Warsaw ghetto. The gas chambers couldn't handle the load. The small gas chambers. The Jews had to wait their turn for a day, two days, three days. They foresaw what was coming. They foresaw it. They may not have been certain, but many knew. There were Jewish women who slashed their daughters' wrists at night, then cut their own. Others poisoned themselves.

They heard the engine feeding the gas chamber. A tank engine was used in that gas chamber. At Treblinka the only gas used was engine exhaust. Zyklon gas—that was Auschwitz.

Because of the delay, Eberl, the camp commandant, phoned Lublin and said: "We can't go on this way. I can't do it any longer. We have to break off." Overnight, Wirth arrived. He inspected everything and then left. He returned with people from Belzec, experts. Wirth arranged to suspend the trains. The corpses lying there were cleared away. That was the period of the old gas chambers. Because there were so many dead that couldn't be gotten rid of, the bodies piled up around the gas chambers and stayed there for days. Under this pile of bodies was a cesspool three inches deep, full of blood, worms and shit. No one wanted to clean it out. The Jews preferred to be shot rather than work there.

Preferred to be shot?

It was awful. Burying their own people, seeing it all. The dead flesh came off in their hands. So Wirth went there himself with a few Germans and had long belts rigged up that were wrapped around the dead torsos to pull them.

Who did that?

SS men and Jews.

Jews too?

Jews too!

What did the Germans do?

They forced the Jews to . . .

They beat them?

. . . or they themselves helped with the cleanup.

Which Germans did that?

Some of our guards who were assigned up there.

The Germans themselves?

They had to.

They were in command!

They were in command, but they were also commanded.

I think the Jews did it.

In that case, the Germans had to lend a hand.

||||||||||||||||||||||||||||||||||||||||||||||||||||||||||||||||||||||||||||||||||||||||||||||||||||||||||||||||||||||||||||||||||||||||||||||||||||||||||||

AUSCHWITZ

Filip Müller, Czech Jew, survivor of the five liquidations of the Auschwitz "special detail"

Filip, on that Sunday in May 1942 when you first entered the Auschwitz 1 crematorium, how old were you?

Twenty. It was a Sunday in May. We were locked in an

underground cell in Block 11. We were held in secret. Then some SS men appeared and marched us along a street in the camp. We went through a gate, and around three hundred feet away, three hundred feet from the gate, I suddenly saw a

building. It had a flat roof and a smokestack. I saw a door in the rear. I thought they were taking us to be shot. Suddenly, before a door, under a lamp in the middle of this building, a young SS man told us: "Inside, filthy swine!" We entered a corridor. They drove us along it. Right away, the stench, the smoke choked me. They kept on chasing us, and then I made out the shapes of the first two ovens. Between the ovens some Jewish prisoners were working. We were in the incineration chamber of the crematorium in Camp 1 at Auschwitz.

From there they herded us to another big room and told us to undress the corpses. I looked around me. There were hundreds of bodies, all dressed. Piled with the corpses were suitcases, bundles and, scattered everywhere, strange, bluish purple crystals. I couldn't understand any of it. It was like a blow on the head, as if I'd been stunned. I didn't even know where I was. Above all, I couldn't understand how they managed to kill so many people at once.

When we undressed some of them, the order was given to feed the ovens. Suddenly, an SS man rushed up and told me: "Get out of here! Go stir the bodies!" What did he mean, "Stir the bodies"? I entered the cremation chamber. There was a Jewish prisoner, Fischel, who later became a squad leader. He looked at me, and I watched him poke the fire with a long rod. He told me: "Do as I'm doing, or the SS will kill you." I picked up a steel poker and did as he was doing. I obeyed Fischel's order. At that point I was in shock, as if I'd been hypnotized, ready to do whatever I was told. I was so mindless, so horrified, that I did everything Fischel told me. So the ovens were fed, but we were so inexperienced that we left the fans on too long. There were fans to make the fire hotter. They worked too long. The firebrick suddenly exploded, blocking the pipes linking the Auschwitz crematorium with the smokestack. Cremation was interrupted. The ovens were out of action.

That evening some trucks came, and we had to load the rest, some three hundred bodies, into the trucks. Then we were taken . . . I still don't know where, but probably to a field at Birkenau. We were ordered to unload the bodies and put them in a pit. There was a ditch, an artificial pit. Suddenly, water gushed up from underground and swept the bodies down. When night came, we had to stop that horrible work. We were loaded into the trucks and returned to Auschwitz.

The next day we were taken to the same place, but the water had risen. Some SS men came with a fire truck and pumped out the water. We had to go down into that muddy pit to stack up the bodies. But they were slimy. For example,

I grasped a woman, but her hands . . . her hand was slippery, slimy. I tried to pull her, but I fell over backward, into the water, the mud. It was the same for all of us. Up top, at the edge of the pit, Aumeyer and Grabner yelled: "Get cracking, you filth, you bastards! We'll show you, you bunch of shits!" And in these . . . call them . . . circumstances, two of my companions couldn't take any more. One was a French student. All Jews! They were exhausted. They just lay there in the mud. Aumeyer called one of his SS men: "Go on, finish off those swine!" They were exhausted. And they were shot in the pit.

There were no crematoriums at Birkenau then?

No, there weren't any there yet. Birkenau still wasn't completely set up. Only Camp B1, which was later the women's camp, existed. It wasn't until the spring of 1943 that skilled workmen, and unskilled laborers, all Jews, must have gone to work here and built the four crematoriums. Each crematorium had fifteen ovens, a big undressing room of around three thousand square feet, and a big gas chamber where up to three thousand people at once could be gassed.

T R E B L I N K A

Franz Suchomel

The new gas chambers were built in September 1942.

Who built them?

Hackenhold and Lambert supervised the Jews who did the work, the bricklaying at least. Ukrainian carpenters made the doors. The gas-chamber doors themselves were armored bunker doors. I think they were brought from Bialystok, from some Russian bunkers.

What was the capacity of the new gas chambers? There were two of them, right?

Yes. But the old ones hadn't been demolished. When there were a lot of trains, a lot of people, the old ones were put back into service. And here . . . the Jews say there were five on each side. I say there were four, but I'm not sure. In any case, only the upper row on this side was in action.

Why not the other side?

Disposing of the bodies would have been too complicated.

Too far?

Yes. Up there Wirth had built the death camp, assigning a detail of Jewish workers to it. The detail had a fixed number in it, around two hundred people, who worked only in the death camp.

But what was the capacity of the new gas chambers?

The new gas chambers . . . Let's see . . . They could finish off three thousand people in two hours.

How many people at once in a single gas chamber?

I can't say exactly. The Jews say two hundred. Imagine a room this size.

They put more in at Auschwitz.

Auschwitz was a factory!

And Treblinka?

I'll give you my definition. Keep this in mind! Treblinka was a primitive but efficient production line of death. Understand?

Yes. But primitive?

Primitive, yes. But it worked well, that production line of death.

Was Belzec even more rudimentary?

Belzec was the laboratory. Wirth was camp commandant. He tried everything imaginable there. He got off on the wrong foot. The pits were overflowing and the cesspool seeped out in front of the SS mess hall. It stank—in front of the mess hall, in front of their barracks.

Were you at Belzec?

No. Wirth with his own men—with Franz, with Oberhauser

and Hackenhold—he tried everything there. Those three had to put the bodies in the pits themselves so that Wirth could see how much space he needed. And when they rebelled—Franz refused—Wirth beat Franz with a whip. He whipped Hackenhold too. You see?

Kurt Franz?

Kurt Franz. That's how Wirth was. Then, with that experience behind him, he came to Treblinka.

||||||||||||||||||||||||||||||||||||||||||||||||||||||||||||||||||||||||||||||||||||||||||||||||||||||||||||||||||||||||||||||||||||||||||

B E L Z E C

Joseph Oberhauser (Munich), in a beer hall

Excuse me. How many quarts of beer a day do you sell? You can't tell me?

I'd rather not. I have my reasons.

But why not? How many quarts of beer a day do you sell?

||||||||||||||||||||||||||||||| _____

Another bartender in the beer hall

Go on, tell him.

Joseph Oberhauser

Tell him what?

The other bartender

Just tell him approximately.

Joseph Oberhauser

Four hundred, five hundred quarts.

That's a lot! Have you worked here long?

Around twenty years.

Why are you hiding your face?

I have my reasons.

What reasons?

Never mind.

Do you recognize this man? No? Christian Wirth? Mr. Ober-
hauser! Do you remember Belzec? No memories of Belzec? Of the
overflowing graves? You don't remember?

T R E B L I N K A

**Alfred Spiess, German state prosecutor at the
Treblinka trial (Frankfurt, 1960)**

When the Aktion itself first got under way, it was almost
totally improvised. At Treblinka, for example, the commandant, Eberl, let more trains come in than the camp could
handle. It was a disaster! Mountains of corpses! Word of this
foul-up reached the head of the Aktion Reinhard, Odilo Globocznik, in Lublin. He went to Treblinka to see what was
happening. There's a very concrete account of the trip by his
former driver, Oberhauser. Globocznik arrived on a hot day in
August. The camp was permeated with the stench of rotting
flesh. Globocznik didn't even bother to enter the camp. He
stopped here, before the commandant's barracks, sent for Eberl
and greeted him with these words: "How dare you accept so
many every day when you can only process three thousand?"
Operations were suspended, Eberl was transferred and Wirth
came, followed immediately by Stangl, and the camp was completely reorganized.

The Aktion Reinhard covered three extermination camps:
Treblinka, Sobibor and Belzec. There's also talk of three death

camps on the Bug River, for they were all located on or near
the Bug. The gas chambers were the heart of the camp. They
were built first, in a wood, or in a field, as at Treblinka. The
gas chambers were the only stone buildings. All the others
were wooden sheds. These camps weren't built to last.
Himmler was in a hurry to begin the "final solution." The
Germans had to capitalize on their eastward advance . . . and
use this remote back country to carry out their mass murder
as secretly as possible. So at first they couldn't manage the
perfection they achieved three months later.

S O B I B O R

Jan Piwonski

Near the end of March 1942, sizable groups of Jews were
herded here, groups of fifty to one hundred people. Several
trains arrived with sections of barracks, with posts, barbed
wire, bricks, and construction of the camp as such began. The
Jews unloaded these cars and carted the sections of barracks to
the camp. The Germans made them work extremely fast. Seeing the pace they worked at—it was extremely brutal—and
seeing the complex being built, and the fence, which, after all,

enclosed a vast space, we realized that what the Germans were building wasn't meant to aid mankind.

Early in June the first convoy arrived. I'd say there were over forty cars. With the convoy were SS men in black uniforms. It happened one afternoon. I had just finished work. But I got on my bicycle and went home.

Why?

I merely thought these people had come to build the camp, as the others had before them. That convoy—there was no way of knowing that it was the first earmarked for extermination. Besides, one couldn't have known that Sobibor would be used for the mass extermination of the Jewish people. The next morning when I came here to work, the station was absolutely silent, and we realized, after talking with the other railway men who worked at the station here, that something utterly incomprehensible had happened. First of all, when the camp was being built, there were orders shouted in German, there were screams, Jews were working at a run, there were shots, and here there was that silence, no work crews, a really total silence. Forty cars had arrived, and then . . . nothing. It was all very strange.

It was the silence that tipped them off?

That's right.

Can he describe that silence?

It was a silence . . . a standstill in the camp. You heard and saw nothing; nothing moved. So then they began to wonder, "Where have they put those Jews?"

A U S C H W I T Z

Filip Müller

Cell 13, Block 11 at Auschwitz 1 is where the "special work detail" was held. The cell was underground, isolated. For we were "bearers of secrets," we were reprieved dead men. We weren't allowed to talk to anyone, or contact any prisoner, or even the SS. Only those in charge of the Aktion.

There was a window. We heard what happened in the courtyard. The executions, the victims' cries, the screams, but we couldn't see anything. This went on for several days.

One night an SS man came from the political section. It was around 4 A.M. The whole camp was still asleep. There wasn't a sound in the camp. We were again taken out of our cell, and led to the crematorium. There for the first time I saw the procedure used with those who came in alive. We were lined up against a wall and told: "No one may talk to those people." Suddenly, the wooden door to the crematorium courtyard opened, and two hundred and fifty to three hundred people filed in—old people and women. They carried bundles, wore the Star of David. Even from a distance I could tell they were

Polish Jews, probably from Upper Silesia, from the Sosnowitz ghetto, some twenty miles from Auschwitz. I caught some of the things they said. I heard *fachowitz,* meaning "skilled worker." And *Malach-ha-Mawis,* which means "the Angel of Death" in Yiddish. Also, *Harginnen:* "They're going to kill us." From what I could hear, I clearly understood the struggle going on inside them. Sometimes they spoke of work, probably hoping that they'd be put to work. Or they spoke of *Malach-ha-Mawis,* The Angel of Death. The conflicting words echoed the conflict in their feelings. Then a sudden silence fell over those gathered in the crematorium courtyard. All eyes converged on the flat roof of the crematorium. Who was standing there? Aumeyer, the SS man, Grabner, the head of the political section, and Hössler, the SS officer. Aumeyer addressed the crowd: "You're here to work for our soldiers fighting at the front. Those who can work will be all right."

It was obvious that hope flared in those people. You could feel it clearly. The executioners had gotten past the first obstacle. He saw it was succeeding. Then Grabner spoke up: "We need masons, electricians, all the trades." Next, Hössler took over. He pointed to a short man in the crowd. I can still see him. "What's your trade?" The man said: "Mr. Officer, I'm a tailor." "A tailor? What kind of a tailor?" "A man's . . . No, for both men and women." "Wonderful: We need people like you in our workshops." Then he questioned a woman: "What's your trade?" "Nurse," she replied. "Splendid! We need nurses in our hospitals, for our soldiers. We need all of you! But first, undress. You must be disinfected. We want you healthy." I could see the people were calmer, reassured by what they'd heard, and they began to undress. Even if they still had their doubts, if you want to live, you must hope. Their clothing remained in the courtyard, scattered everywhere. Aumeyer was beaming, very proud of how he'd handled things. He turned to some of the SS men and told them: "You

see? That's the way to do it!" By this device a great leap
forward had been made! now the clothing could be used.

||||||||||||||||||||||||||||||||||||||||||||||||||||||||||||||||||||||||||||||||||||||||||||||||||||||||||||||||||||||||||||||||||||||||||||||||||||||||||||||

Raul Hilberg, historian (Burlington, Vermont)

In all of my work I have never begun by asking the big questions, because I was always afraid that I would come up with
small answers; and I have preferred to address these things
which are minutiae or details in order that I might then be able
to put together in a gestalt a picture which, if not an explanation, is at least a description, a more full description, of what
transpired. And in that sense I look also at the bureaucratic
destruction process—for this is what it was—as a series of
minute steps taken in logical order and relying above all as
much as possible on experience. And this goes not only, incidentally, for the administrative steps that were taken, but also
the psychological arguments, even the propaganda. Amazingly
little was newly invented till of course the moment came when
one had to go beyond that which had already been established
by precedent, that one had to gas these people or in some sense
annihilate them on a large scale. Then these bureaucrats became inventors. But like all inventors of institutions they did
not copyright or patent their achievements, and they prefer
obscurity.

What did they get from the past, the Nazis?

They got the actual content of measures which they took. For example, the barring of Jews from office, the prohibition of intermarriages and of the employment in Jewish homes of female persons under the age of forty-five, the various marking decrees—especially the Jewish star—the compulsory ghetto, the voidance of any will executed by a Jew that might work in such a way as to prevent inheritance of his property by someone who was a Christian. Many such measures had been worked out over the course of more than a thousand years by authorities of the church and by secular governments that followed in those footsteps. And the experience gathered over that time became a reservoir that could be used, and which indeed was used to an amazing extent. One can compare a rather large number of German laws with their counterparts in the past and find complete parallels, even in detail, as if there were a memory which automatically extended to the period of 1933, 1935, 1939 and beyond.

They invented very little, and they did not invent the portrait of the Jew, which also was taken over lock, stock and barrel from writings going back to the sixteenth century. So even the propaganda, the realm of imagination and invention —even there they were remarkably in the footsteps of those who preceded them, from Martin Luther to the nineteenth century. And here again they were not inventive.

They had to become inventive with the "final solution." That was their great invention, and that is what made this entire process different from all others that had preceded that event. In this respect, what transpired when the "final solution" was adopted—or, to be more precise, bureaucracy moved into it—was a turning point in history. Even here I would suggest a logical progression, one that came to fruition in what might be called closure, because from the earliest days, from the fourth century, the sixth century, the missionaries of Christianity had said in effect to the Jews: "You may not live among us as Jews." The secular rulers who followed them from the late Middle Ages then decided: "You may not live among us," and the Nazis finally decreed: "You may not live." Conversion was followed by expulsion, and the third was the territorial solution, which was of course the solution carried out in the territories under German command, excluding emigration: death. The "final solution." And the "final solution," you see, is really final, because people who are converted can yet be Jews in secret, people who are expelled can yet return. But people who are dead will not reappear.

In such a respect—the last stage—they were really pioneers and inventors?

This was something unprecedented, and this was something new.

How can one give some idea about this complete newness, because it was new for them too?

Yes, it was new, and I think for this reason one cannot find a specific document, a specific planned outline or blueprint which stated: "Now the Jews will be killed." Everything is left to inference from general words. General words—the very wording "final solution" or "total solution" or "territorial solution" leaves something to the bureaucrat that he must infer. He cannot read that document. One cannot even read Göring's famous letter to Heydrich at the end of July 1941 charging him in two paragraphs to proceed with the "final solution," and examining that document, consider that everything is clarified. Far from it. It was an authorization to invent. It was an authorization to begin something that was not as yet capable of being put into words. I think of it that way.

It was a case for every agency as a matter of fact?

Absolutely for every agency. In every aspect of this operation, invention was necessary. Certainly at this point, because every problem was unprecedented. Not just how to kill the Jews, but what to do with their property thereafter. And not only that, but how to deal with the problem of not letting the world know what had happened. All this multitude of problems was new.

‖‖

C H E L M N O

Franz Schalling (Germany)

First, explain to me how you came to Kulmhof, to Chelmno. You were at Lodz, right?

In Lodz, yes. In Litzmannstadt. We were on permanent guard duty. Protecting military objectives: mills, the roads, when Hitler went to East Prussia. It was dreary, and we were told:

"We need men who want to break out of this routine." So we volunteered. We were issued winter uniforms, overcoats, fur hats, fur-lined boots, and two or three days later we were told: "We're off!" We were put aboard two or three trucks . . . I don't know . . . they had benches, and we rode and rode. Finally, we arrived. The place was crawling with SS men and police. Our first question was "What goes on here?" They said: "You'll find out!"

You weren't in the SS, you were . . .

Police.

Which police?

Security guards. We were told to report to the Deutsches Haus, German headquarters, the only big stone building in the village. We were taken into it. An SS man immediately told us: "This is a top-secret mission!

Secret?

"A top-secret mission." "Sign this!" We each had to sign. There was a form ready for each of us, a pledge of secrecy. We never even got to read it through.

You had to take an oath?

No, just sign, promising to shut up about whatever we'd see. Not say a word. After we'd signed, we were told: "Final solution of the Jewish question." We didn't understand what that meant. It all looked normal.

So someone said . . .

He told us what was going to happen there.

Someone said: "The final solution of the Jewish question"? You'd be assigned to the "final solution"?

Yes, but what did that mean? We'd never heard that before. So it was explained to us.

Just when was this?

Let's see . . . when was it . . . ? In the winter of 1941–42. Then we were assigned to our stations. Our guard post was at the side of the road, a sentry box in front of the castle.

So you were in the "castle detail"?

That's right.

Can you describe what you saw?

We could see. We were at the gatehouse. When the Jews arrived, the way they looked! Half frozen, starved, dirty, already half dead. Old people, children. Think of it! The long trip here, standing in a truck, packed in! Who knows if they knew what was in store! They didn't trust anyone, that's for sure. After months in the ghetto, you can imagine! I heard an SS man shout at them: "You're going to be deloused and have a bath. You're going to work here." The Jews consented. They said: "Yes, that's what we want to do."

Was the castle big?

Pretty big, with huge front steps. The SS man stood at the top of the steps.

Then what happened?

They were hustled into two or three big rooms on the first floor. They had to undress, give up everything: rings, gold, everything.

How long did the Jews stay there?

Long enough to undress. Then, stark naked, they had to run down more steps to an underground corridor that led back up to the ramp, where the gas van awaited them.

Did the Jews enter the van willingly?

No, they were beaten. Blows fell everywhere, and the Jews understood. They screamed. It was frightful! Frightful! I know because we went down to the cellar when they were all in the van. We opened the cells of the work detail, the Jewish workers who collected stuff thrown into the yard out of a first-floor window.

Describe the gas vans.

They stretched, say, from here to the window. Just big trucks, like moving vans, with two rear doors.

What system was used? How did they kill them?

With exhaust fumes. It went like this. A Pole yelled "Gas!" Then the driver got under the van to hook up the pipe that fed the gas into the van.

Yes, but how?

From the motor.

Yes, but through what?

A pipe—a tube. He fiddled around under the truck, I'm not sure how.

It was just exhaust gas?

That's all.

Who were the drivers?

SS men. All those men were SS.

Were there many of these drivers?

I don't know.

Were there two, three, five, ten?

Not that many. Two or three, that's all. I think there were two vans, one big, one smaller.

Did the driver sit in the cab of the van?

Yes. He climbed into the cab after the doors were shut and started the motor.

Did he race the motor?

I don't know.

Could you hear the sound of the motor?

Yes, from the gate we could hear it turn over.

Was it a loud noise?

The noise of a truck engine.

The van was stationary while the motor ran?

That's right. Then it started moving. We opened the gate and it headed for the woods.

Were the people already dead?

I don't know. It was quiet, No more screams. You couldn't hear anything as they drove by.

Michael Podchlebnik, survivor of the first period of extermination at Chelmno (Kulmhof), the "castle period"

He recalls that it was 1941, two days before the New Year. They were routed out at night, and in the morning they reached Chelmno. There was a castle there. When he entered the castle courtyard, he knew something awful was going on. He already understood. They saw clothes and shoes scattered in the courtyard. Yet they were alone there. He knew his parents had been through there, and there wasn't a Jew left. They were taken down into a cellar. On a wall was written "No one leaves here alive." Graffiti in Yiddish. There were lots of names. He thinks it was the Jews from villages around

Chelmno who had come before him who had written their
names. A few days after New Year's they heard people arrive
in a truck one morning. The people were taken out of the truck

and up to the first floor of the castle. The Germans lied, saying
they were to be deloused. They were chased down the other
side, where a van was waiting. The Germans pushed and beat
them with their weapons to hustle them into the trucks faster.
He heard people praying—*Shema Israël*—and he heard the
van's rear doors being shut. Their screams were heard, becoming fainter and fainter, and when there was total silence, the
van left. He and the four others were brought out of the cellar.
They went upstairs and gathered up the clothes remaining
outside the supposed baths.

Did he understand then how they'd died?

Yes, first because there had been rumors of it. And when he went out, he saw the sealed vans, so he knew. He understood that people were gassed because he'd heard the screams, and heard how they weakened, and later the vans were taken into the woods.

What were the vans like?

Like the ones that deliver cigarettes here. They were enclosed, with double-leaf rear doors.

What color?

The color the Germans used—green, ordinary.

Mrs. Michelsohn (Germany), wife of a Nazi schoolteacher in Chelmno

How many German families lived in Chelmno, Kulmhof?

Ten or eleven, I'd say. Germans from Wolhnia and two families from the Reich—the Bauers and us, the Michelsohns.

How did you wind up in Kulmhof?

I was born in Laage, and I was sent to Kulmhof. They were looking for volunteer settlers, and I signed up. That's how I got there. First in Warthbrücken (Kolo), then Chelmno, Kulmhof.

Directly from Laage?

No, I left from Münster.

Did you opt to go to Kulmhof?

No, I asked for Wartheland.

Why?

A pioneering spirit.

You were young?

Oh, yes, I was young.

You wanted to be useful?

Yes.

What was your first impression of Wartheland?

It was primitive. Worse than primitive.

Difficult to understand, right? But why . . . ?

The sanitary facilities were disastrous. The only toilet was in Warthbrücken, in the town hall; you had to go there. The rest was a disaster.

Why a disaster?

There were no toilets at all! There were privies. I can't tell you how primitive it was.

Astonishing! Why did you choose such a primitive place?

Oh, when you're young, you'll try anything. You can't imagine such places exist. You don't believe it. But that's how it was.

This was the whole village. A very small village, straggling along the road. Just a few houses. There was the church, the castle, a store too, the administrative building and the school. The castle was next to the church, with a high board fence around both.

How far was your house from the church?

It was just opposite—150 feet.

Did you see the gas vans?

No . . . Yes, from the outside. They shuttled back and forth. I never looked inside; I didn't see Jews in them. I only saw things from outside—the Jews' arrival, their disposition, how they were loaded aboard. Since World War I the castle had been in ruins. Only part of it could still be used. That's where the Jews were taken. This ruined castle was used for housing and delousing the Poles, and so on.

The Jews!

Yes, the Jews.

Why do you call them Poles and not Jews?

Sometimes I get them mixed up.

There's a difference between Poles and Jews?

Oh yes!

What difference?

The Poles weren't exterminated, and the Jews were. That's the difference. An external difference.

And the inner difference?

I can't assess that. I don't know enough about psychology and anthropology. The difference between the Poles and the Jews? Anyway, they couldn't stand each other.

‖‖‖

C H E L M N O

Claude Lanzmann reads a letter in front of a building that was formerly the Grabow synagogue. On January 19, 1942, the rabbi of Grabow, Jacob Schulmann, wrote the following letter to his friends in Lodz:

"My very dear friends, I waited to write to confirm what I'd heard. Alas, to our great grief, we now know all. I spoke to an eyewitness who escaped. He told me everything. They're exterminated in Chelmno, near Dombie, and they're all buried in Rzuszow forest. The Jews are killed in two ways: by shooting or gas. It's just happened to thousands of Lodz Jews. Do not think that this is being written by a madman. Alas, it is the tragic, horrible truth.

" 'Horror, horror! Man, shed thy clothes, cover thy head with ashes, run in the streets and dance in thy madness.' I am so weary that my pen can no longer write. Creator of the universe, help us!"

The Creator did not help the Jews of Grabow. With their rabbi, they all died in the gas vans at Chelmno a few weeks later. Chelmno is only twelve miles from Grabow.

A group of women

Were there a lot of Jews here in Grabow?

A lot, quite a few. They were sent to Chelmno.

Has she always lived near the synagogue?

Yes. The Poles' word is *buzinica,* not synagogue. She says it's now a furniture warehouse, but they didn't harm it from a religious point of view. It hasn't been desecrated.

Does she remember the rabbi at the synagogue?

She says she's eighty now and her memory isn't too good, and the Jews have been gone for forty years.

A couple

Barbara, tell this couple they live in a lovely house. Do they agree? Do they think it's a lovely house?

Yes.

Tell me about the decoration of this house, the doors. What does it mean?

People used to do carvings like that.

Did they decorate it that way?

No, it was the Jews again. The door's a good century old.

Did Jews own this house?

Yes, all these houses on the square were Jewish. Jews lived in all the ones in front, on the street.

Where did the Poles live?

In the courtyards, where the privies were.

There used to be a store here. A food store.

Owned by Jews?

Yes.

So the Jews lived in the front, and the Poles in the courtyard, with the privies. How long have these two lived here?

Fifteen years.

Where'd they live before?

In a courtyard across the square.

They've gotten rich?

Yes.

How did they get rich?

They worked.

How old's the gentleman?

He's seventy.

He looks young and hale. Do they remember the Jews of Grabow?

Yes. And when they were deported too. He says he speaks "Jew" well. As a kid he played with Jews, so he speaks "Jew."
    First, they grouped them there, where that restaurant is, or in this square, and took their gold. An elder among the Jews collected the gold and turned it over to the police. That done, the Jews were put in the Catholic Church.

A lot of gold?

Yes, the Jews had gold, and some handsome candelabra.

A man

Did the Poles know the Jews would be killed at Chelmno?

Yes, they knew. The Jews knew it too.

Did the Jews try to do something about it, to rebel, to escape?

The young tried to run away. But the Germans caught them and maybe killed them even more savagely. In every town and village, two or three streets were closed and the Jews kept under guard. They couldn't leave there. Then they were locked in the Polish church here in Grabow, and later taken to Chelmno.

The couple

The Germans threw children as small as these into the trucks by the legs. Old folks too.

The Poles knew the Jews would be gassed in Chelmno? Did this gentleman know?

Yes.

Another man

Does he recall the Jews' deportation from Grabow?

At that time, he worked in the mill, there, opposite, and they saw it all.

What did he think of it? Was it a sad sight?

Yes, it was sad to watch. Nothing to be cheery about.

What trades were the Jews in?

They were tanners, tradesmen, tailors. They sold things— eggs, chickens, butter.

The first man

There were a lot of tailors—tradesmen too. But most were tanners. They had beards and sidelocks. He says they weren't pretty. They stank too, because they were tanners, and the hides stank.

A group of women

The Jewish women were beautiful. The Poles liked to make love with them.

Are Polish women glad there are no Jewesses left?

She said that the women who are her age now also liked to make love.

So the Jewish women were competitors?

It's crazy how the Poles liked the little Jewesses!

Do the Poles miss the little Jewesses?

Naturally, such beautiful women!

Why? What made them so beautiful?

It was because they did nothing. Polish women worked. Jewish women only thought of their beauty and clothes.

So Jewesses did no work!

None at all. They were rich. The Poles had to serve them and work.

I heard her use the word "capital."

The capital was in the hands of the Jews.

Yes. You didn't translate that. Ask her again. The capital was in the Jews' hands?

All Poland was in the Jews' hands.

The first man

Are they glad there are no more Jews here, or sad?

It doesn't bother them. As you know, Jews and Germans ran all Polish industry before the war.

Did they like them, on the whole?

Not much. Above all, they were dishonest.

Was life in Grabow more fun when the Jews were here?

He'd rather not say.

Why does he call them dishonest?

They exploited the Poles. That's what they lived off.

How did they exploit them?

By imposing their prices.

A woman

Ask her if she likes her house.

Yes, but her children live in much better houses. In modern houses! They've all gone to college. Her children are the best educated in the village.

Very good, Madam! Long live education! Isn't this a very old house?

Yes, Jews lived here before.

Did she know them?

Yes.

What was their name?

Benkel, their name was. They had a butcher shop.

Why is she laughing?

Because the gentleman said it was a butcher shop where you could buy cheap meat. Beef!

The first man

What does he think about their being gassed in trucks?

He says he doesn't like that at all. If they'd gone to Israel of their own free will, he might have been glad, but their being killed was unpleasant.

The other man

Does he miss the Jews?

Yes, because there were some beautiful Jewesses. For the young, it was fine.

The group of women

Are they sorry the Jews are no longer here, or pleased?

How can I tell? I never went to school. I can only think of how I am now. Now I'm fine.

Is she better off?

Before the war she picked potatoes. Now she sells eggs and she's much better off.

Because the Jews are gone, or because of socialism?

She doesn't care; she's happy because she's doing well now.

The couple

How did he feel about losing his classmates?

It still upsets him.

Does he miss the Jews?

Certainly. They were good Jews, Madam says.

Mrs. Michelsohn

The Jews came in trucks, and later there was a narrow-gauge railway that they arrived on. They were packed tightly in the trucks, or in the cars of the narrow-gauge railway. Lots of women and children. Men too, but most of them were old.

The strongest were put in work details. They walked with chains on their legs. In the morning they fetched water, looked for food, and so on. These weren't killed right away. That was done later. I don't know what became of them. They didn't survive, anyway.

Two of them did.

Only two.

They were in chains?

On the legs.

All of them?

The workers, yes. The others were killed at once.

The Jewish work squad went through the village in chains?

Yes.

Could people speak to them?

No, that was impossible. No one dared.

No one dared. Why? Was it dangerous?

Yes, there were guards. Anyway, people wanted nothing to do with all that. Do you see? Gets on your nerves, seeing that every day. You can't force a whole village to watch such distress! When the Jews arrived, when they were pushed into the church or the castle . . . And the screams! It was frightful! Depressing. Day after day, the same spectacle! It was terrible. A sad sight. They screamed. They knew what was happening. At first the Jews thought they were going to be deloused. But they soon understood. Their screams grew wilder and wilder.

Horrifying screams. Screams of terror! Because they knew what was happening to them.

Do you know how many Jews were exterminated there?

Four something. Four hundred thousand, forty thousand.

Four hundred thousand.

Four hundred thousand, yes. I knew it had a four in it. Sad, sad, sad!

Simon Srebnik

> "When the soldiers march along
> the girls open their doors and windows."

Mrs. Michelsohn

Do you remember a Jewish child, a boy of thirteen? He was in the work squad. He sang on the river.

On the Narew River?

Yes.

Is he still alive?

Yes, he's alive. He sang a German song that the SS in Chelmno taught him. "When the soldiers march, . . .

". . . the girls open their windows and doors . . ."

Group of villagers before the church in Chelmno, around Simon Srebnik

So it's a holiday in Chelmno?

Yes.

What holiday? What's being celebrated?

The birth of the Virgin Mary. It's her birthday.

It's a huge crowd, isn't it?

But the weather's bad—it's raining.

Are they glad to see Srebnik again?

Very. It's a great pleasure. They're glad to see him again because they know all he's lived through. Seeing him as he is now, they're very pleased.

Why does the whole village remember him?

They remember him well because he walked with chains on

his ankles, and he sang on the river. He was young, he was skinny, he looked ready for his coffin. Ripe for a coffin!

Did he seem happy or sad?

Even the lady, when she saw that child, she told the German: "Let that child go!" He asked her: "Where to?" "To his father and mother." Looking at the sky, he said: "He'll soon go to them."

They remember when the Jews were locked in this church?

Yes, they do. They brought them to the church in trucks. All day long and into the night.

What happened? Can they describe it in detail?

At first, the Jews were taken to the castle. Only later were they put into the church.

Yes, in the second phase.

In the morning they were taken into the woods in very big armored vans. The gas came through the bottom.

Then they were carried in gas vans, weren't they?

Yes, in gas vans.

Where did the vans pick them up?

The Jews?

Yes.

Here, at the church door. They went right to the door.

The vans came to the church door! They all knew these were death vans, to gas people?

Yes, they couldn't help knowing.

They heard screams at night?

The Jews moaned, they were hungry. They were shut in and starved.

Did they have any food?

You couldn't look there. You couldn't talk to a Jew. Even going by on the road, you couldn't look there.

Did they look anyway?

Yes, vans came and the Jews were moved farther off. You could see them, but on the sly. In sidelong glances.

What kinds of cries and moans were heard at night?

They called on Jesus and Mary and God, sometimes in German, as she puts it.

The Jews called on Jesus, Mary and God!

The presbytery was full of suitcases.

The Jews' suitcases?

Yes, and there was gold.

How does she know there was gold? The procession! We'll stop now.

Were there as many Jews in the church as there were Christians today?

Almost.

How many gas vans were needed to empty it out?

An average of fifty.

It took fifty vans to empty it! In a steady stream?

Yes.

The lady said before that the Jews' suitcases were dumped in the house opposite. What was in this baggage?

Pots with false bottoms.

What was in the false bottoms?

Valuables, objects of value. They also had gold in their clothes. When given food, some Jews threw them valuables, some threw money.

They said before it was forbidden to talk to Jews.

Absolutely forbidden.

Do they miss the Jews?

Of course. We wept too, Madam says. And Mr. Kantarowski gave them bread and cucumbers.

Why do they think all this happened to the Jews?

Because they were the richest! Many Poles were also exterminated. Even priests.

Mr. Kantarowski will tell us what a friend told him. It happened in Myndjewyce, near Warsaw.

Go on.

The Jews there were gathered in a square. The rabbi asked an SS man: "Can I talk to them?" The SS man said yes. So the rabbi said that around two thousand years ago the Jews con-demned the innocent Christ to death. And when they did that, they cried out: "Let his blood fall on our heads and on our sons' heads." Then the rabbi told them: "Perhaps the time has come for that, so let us do nothing, let us go, let us do as we're asked."

He thinks the Jews expiated the death of Christ?

He doesn't think so, or even that Christ sought revenge. He didn't say that. The rabbi said it. It was God's will, that's all!

What'd she say?

So Pilate washed his hands and said: "Christ is innocent," and he sent Barrabas. But the Jews cried out: "Let his blood fall on our heads!"

That's all; now you know!

Mr. Falborski

Was the road between the village of Chelmno and the woods where the pits were located asphalted as it is now?

The road was narrower then, but it was asphalted.

How many feet were the pits from the road?

They were around sixteen hundred feet, maybe nineteen hundred or twenty-two hundred feet away, so even from the road, you couldn't see them.

How fast did the vans go?

At moderate speed, kind of slow. It was a calculated speed, because they had to kill the people inside on the way. When they went too fast, the people weren't quite dead on arrival in the woods. By going slower, they had time to kill the people inside. Once a van skidded on a curve. Half an hour later I arrived at the hut of a forest warden named Sendjak. He told me: "Too bad you were late. You could have seen a van that skidded. The rear of the van opened, and the Jews fell out on the road. They were still alive. Seeing those Jews crawling, a Gestapo man took out his revolver and shot them. He finished them all off. Then they brought Jews who were working in the woods. They righted the van and put the bodies back inside."

Simon Srebnik

This was the road the gas vans used. There were eighty people in each van. When they arrived, the SS said: "Open the doors!" We opened them. The bodies tumbled right out. An SS man said, "Two men inside!" These two men worked at the ovens. They were experienced. Another SS man screamed: "Hurry up! The other van's coming!" We worked until the whole shipment was burned. That's how it went, all day long. So it went.

I remember that once they were still alive. The ovens were full, and the people lay on the ground. They were all moving,

they were coming back to life, and when they were thrown
into the ovens, they were all conscious. Alive. They could feel
the fire burn them.

When we built the ovens, I wondered what they were for. An
SS man told me: "To make charcoal. For laundry irons."
That's what he told me. I didn't know. When the ovens were
completed, the logs put in and the gasoline poured on and
lighted, and when the first gas van arrived, then we knew why
the ovens were built.

When I saw all that, it didn't affect me. Neither did the
second or third shipment. I was only thirteen, and all I'd ever
seen until then were dead bodies. Maybe I didn't understand.
Maybe if I'd been older, I'd have understood, but the fact is,
I didn't. I'd never seen anything else. In the ghetto in Lodz I
saw that as soon as anyone took a step, he fell dead. I thought
that's the way things had to be, that it was normal. I'd walk the

streets of Lodz, maybe one hundred yards, and there'd be two hundred bodies. People were hungry. They went into the street and they fell, they fell. Sons took their fathers' bread, fathers took their sons', everyone wanted to stay alive.

So when I came here, to Chelmno, I was already . . . I didn't care about anything. I thought: "If I survive, I just want one thing: five loaves of bread." To eat. That's all. That's what I thought. But I dreamed too that if I survive, I'll be the only one left in the world, not another soul. Just me. One. Only me left in the world, if I get out of here.

Geheime Reichssache (Secret Reich Business)
Berlin, June 5, 1942
Changes for special vehicles now in service at Kulmhof (Chelmno) and for those now being built

Since December 1941, ninety-seven thousand have been processed (*verarbeitet* in German) by the three vehicles in service, with no major incidents. In the light of observations made so far, however, the following technical changes are needed:

The vans' normal load is usually nine per square yard. In Saurer vehicles, which are very spacious, maximum use of space is impossible, not because of any possible overload, but because loading to full capacity would affect the vehicle's stability. So reduction of the load space seems necessary. It must absolutely be reduced by a yard, instead of trying to solve the problem, as hitherto, by reducing the number of pieces loaded. Besides, this extends the operating time, as the empty void must also be filled with carbon monoxide. On the other hand, if the load space is reduced, and the vehicle is packed solid, the operating time can be considerably shortened. The manufacturers told us during a discussion that reducing the size of the van's rear would throw it badly off balance. The front axle, they claim, would be overloaded. In fact, the balance is automatically restored, because the merchandise aboard displays during the operation a natural tendency to rush to the rear doors, and is mainly found lying there at the end of the operation. So the front axle is not overloaded.

2. The lighting must be better protected than now. The lamps must be enclosed in a steel grid to prevent their being damaged. Lights could be eliminated, since they apparently are never used. However, it has been observed that when the doors are shut, the load always presses hard against them [against the doors] as soon as darkness sets in. This is because the load naturally rushes toward the light when darkness sets in, which makes closing the doors difficult. Also, because of the alarming nature of darkness, screaming always occurs when the doors are closed. It would therefore be useful to light the lamp before and during the first moments of the operation.

3. For easy cleaning of the vehicle, there must be a sealed drain in the middle of the floor. The drainage hole's cover, eight to twelve inches in diameter, would be equipped with a slanting trap, so that fluid liquids can drain off during the operation. During cleaning, the drain can be used to evacuate large pieces of dirt.

The aforementioned technical changes are to be made to vehicles in service only when they come in for repairs. As for the ten vehicles ordered from Saurer, they must be equipped with all innovations and changes shown by use and experience to be necessary.

Submitted for decision to Gruppenleiter II D, SS-Obersturmbannführer Walter Rauff.

Signed: Just

||||||||||||||||||||||||||||||||||||||||||||||||||||||||||||||||||||||||||||||||||||||||||||||||||||||||||||||||||||||||||||||||||||||||||||||||||||||||||||

T R E B L I N K A

Franz Suchomel

"Looking squarely ahead, brave and joyous,
at the world,
the squads march to work.
All that matters to us now is Treblinka.
It is our destiny.
That's why we've become one with Treblinka
in no time at all.
We know only the word of our commander,
we know only obedience and duty,
we want to serve, to go on serving,
until a little luck ends it all. Hurray!"

Once more, but louder!

We're laughing about it, but it's so sad!

No one's laughing.

Don't be sore at me. You want history—I'm giving you history. Franz wrote the words. The melody came from Buchenwald. Camp Buchenwald, where Franz was a guard. New Jews who arrived in the morning, new "worker Jews," were taught the song. And by evening they had to be able to sing along with it.

Sing it again.

All right.

It's very important. But loud!

> "Looking squarely ahead, brave and joyous,
>   at the world,
>   the squads march to work.
>   All that matters to us now is Treblinka.
>   It is our destiny.
>   That's why we've become one with Treblinka
>   in no time at all.
>   We know only the word of our Commander,
>   we know only obedience and duty,
>   we want to serve, to go on serving,
>   until a little luck ends it all. Hurray!"

Satisfied? That's unique. No Jew knows that today!

How was it possible in Treblinka in peak days to "process" eighteen thousand people?

Eighteen thousand is too high.

But I read that figure in court reports.

Sure.

To "process" eighteen thousand people, to liquidate them. . . .

Mr. Lanzmann, that's an exaggeration. Believe me.

How many?

Twelve thousand to fifteen thousand. But we had to spend half the night at it. In January the trains started arriving at 6 A.M.

Always at 6 A.M.?

Not always. Often. The schedules were erratic. Sometimes one came at 6 A.M., then another at noon, maybe another late in the evening. You see?

So a train arrived. I'd like you to describe in detail the whole process during the peak period.

The trains left Malkinia station for Treblinka station. It was about six miles. Treblinka was a village. A small village. As a station, it gained in importance because of the transport of Jews. Thirty to fifty cars would arrive. They were divided into sections of ten or twelve or fifteen cars and shunted into Treblinka Camp and brought to the ramp. The other cars waited, loaded with people, in the Treblinka station. The windows were closed off with barbed wire so no one could get out. On the roofs were the "hellhounds," the Ukrainians or Latvians. The Latvians were the worst. On the ramp, for each car, there stood two Jews from the Blue Squad to speed things up. They said: "Get out, get out. Hurry, hurry!" There were also Ukrainians and Germans.

How many Germans?

From three to five.

No more?

No more. I can assure you.

How many Ukrainians?

Ten.

Ten Ukrainians, five Germans. Two, that is, twenty people from the Blue Squad.

Men from the Blue Squad were here, and here they sent the people inside. The Red Squad was here.

What was the Red Squad's job?

The clothes! To carry the clothes taken off by the men and by the women up here immediately.

How long was it between the unloading at the ramp and the undressing, how many minutes?

For the women let's say an hour in all. An hour, an hour and a half. A whole train took two hours. In two hours it was all over.

Between the time of arrival . . .

and death . . .

. . . it was all over in two hours?

Two hours, two and a half hours, three hours.

A whole train?

Yes, a whole train.

And for only one section, for ten cars, how long?

I can't calculate that, because the sections came one after another and people flooded in constantly, understand? Usually, the men waiting who sat there, or there, were sent straight up via the "funnel." The women were sent last. At the end. They had to go up there too, and often waited here. Five at a time. Fifty people—sixty women with children. They had to wait here until there was room here. Naked! In summer and winter.

Winter in Treblinka can be very cold.

Well, in winter, in December, anyway after Christmas. But even before Christmas it was cold as hell. Between fifteen and minus four. I know: at first it was cold as hell for us too. We didn't have suitable uniforms.

But it was colder . . .

. . . for those poor people . . .

. . . in the "funnel."

In the "funnel" it was very, very cold.

Can you describe this "funnel" precisely? What was it like? How wide? How was it for the people in this "funnel"?

It was about thirteen feet wide, as wide as this room. On each side were palisades this high . . . or this high.

Walls?

No, barbed wire. Woven into the barbed wire were branches of pine trees. You understand? It was known as "camouflage." There was a Camouflage Squad of twenty Jews. They brought in new branches every day from the woods. So everything was screened. People couldn't see anything to the left or right. Nothing. You couldn't see through it. Impossible.

Treblinka, where so many people were exterminated, wasn't big, was it?

It wasn't big. Sixteen hundred feet at the widest point. It wasn't a rectangle, more like a rhomboid. You must realize that here the ground was flat, and here it began to rise. And at the top of the slope was the gas chamber. You had to climb up to it.

The "funnel" was called the "Road to Heaven," wasn't it?

The Jews called it the "Ascension," also the "Last Road." I only heard those two names for it.

I need to see it. The people go into the "funnel." Then what happens? They are totally naked?

Totally naked. Here stood two Ukrainian guards. Mainly for the men. If the men wouldn't go in, they were beaten with whips. The men were "driven" along. Not the women. They weren't beaten.

Why such humanity?

I didn't see it. Maybe they were beaten too.

Why not? They were about to die anyway.

At the entrance to the gas chambers, undoubtedly.

Abraham Bomba

How did it happen? How were you chosen?

There came an order from the Germans to take out the barbers they could get—they need them for a certain job. The job they were needed for we didn't know at that time, but we got together as many barbers as we could.

How long did it happen after your arrival in Treblinka?

This was about four weeks after I was in Treblinka. It was in the morning, around ten o'clock, when a transport came to Treblinka and the women went into the gas chambers. They chose some people from the working people over there, and they asked who was a barber, who was not a barber. I was a barber for quite a number of years, and some of them knew me —people from Czestochowa and other places. So naturally, they chose me and I selected some more barbers who I knew, and we got together.

Professional barbers?

Yes. We got together and were waiting for the order. And the order came to go with them, with the Germans. They took us in to the gas chamber, to the second part of the camp in Treblinka. It was not too far from the first part, and it was all covered with gates, barbed wire and trees covering the gates so that nobody should see there is a gate, or a place going into the gas chamber.

Is that what the Germans call the Schlauch—*the "funnel"?*

No, the Germans called this the "Road to Heaven"—*Himmel-weg.* And we knew about it because we worked for quite a time before going to work in the gas chamber. Going in over there, they put in some benches where the women could sit and not get the idea that this is their last way or the last time they are going to live or breathe or know what is going on.

How long did the barbers cut the hair inside the gas chamber, as that was not always the case?

We worked inside the gas chamber for about a week or ten days. After that they decided that we will cut their hair in the undressing barrack.

How did it look, the gas chamber?

It was not a big room, around twelve feet by twelve feet. But in that room they pushed in a lot of women, almost one on top of another. But like I mentioned before, when we came in, we didn't know what we were going to do. And then one of the kapos came in and said: "Barbers, you have to do a job to make all those women coming in believe that they are just taking a

haircut and going in to take a shower, and from there they go out from this place." We know already that there is no way of going out from this room, because this room was the last place they went in alive, and they will never go out alive again.

Can you describe precisely?

Describe precisely . . . We were waiting there until the transport came in. Women with children pushed in to that place.

We the barbers started to cut their hair, and some of them—
I would say all of them—some of them knew already what was
going to happen to them. We tried to do the best we could—
to be the most human we could.

Excuse me. How did it happen when the women came into the gas
chamber? Were you yourself already in the gas chamber?

I said we were already in the gas chamber, waiting over there
for the transport to come in. Inside the gas chamber—we were
already in.

And suddenly you saw the women comming?

Yes, they came in.

How were they?

They were undressed, naked, without clothes, without anything else—completely naked. All the women and all the children, because they came from the undressing barrack—the
barrack before going into the gas chamber—where they had
undressed themselves.

What did you feel the first time you saw all these naked women?

I felt that accordingly I got to do what they told me, to cut
their hair in a way that it looked like the barber was doing his
job for a woman, and I set out to give them both, to take off
as much hair as I could, because they needed women's hair to
be transported to Germany.

Did you shave them?

No, we didn't. We just cut their hair and made them believe they were getting a nice haircut.

You cut with what—with scissors?

Yes, with scissors and comb, without any clippers. Just like a man's haircut, I would say. Not a boy, to take off all their hair, but just to have the imagination that they're getting a nice haircut.

There were no mirrors?

No, there were no mirrors. There were just benches—not chairs, just benches—where we worked, about sixteen or seventeen barbers, and we had a lot of women in. Every haircut took about two minutes, no more than that because there were a lot of women to come in and get rid of their hair.

Can you imitate how you did it?

How we did it—cut as fast as we could. We were quite a number of us professional barbers, and the way we did it, we just did this and this and we cut this like this here and this side and this side and the hair was all finished. With big movements, naturally, because we did not waste any time. The other party was waiting already outside to do the same thing, the same job.

You said there were about sixteen barbers? You cut the hair of how many women in one batch?

In one day there was about, I would say, going into that place between sixty and seventy women in the same room at one time. After we were finished with this party, another party came in, and there were about 140, 150 women. They were all already taken care of, and they told us to leave the gas chamber for a few minutes, about five minutes, when they put in the gas and choked them to death.

Where did you wait?

We waited outside the gas chamber and on the other side. On this side the women went in and on the other side was a group of working people who took out the dead bodies—some of them were not exactly dead. They took them out, and in two minutes—in one minute—everything was clear. It was clean to take in the other party of women and do the same thing they did to the first one. Most of them had long hair—some had short hair. What we had to do was chop off the hair; like I mentioned, the Germans needed the hair for their purposes.

But I asked you and you didn't answer: What was your impression the first time you saw these naked women arriving with children? What did you feel?

I tell you something. To have a feeling about that . . . it was very hard to feel anything, because working there day and night between dead people, between bodies, your feeling disappeared, you were dead. You had no feeling at all. As a matter of fact, I want to tell you something that happened. At the gas chamber, when I was chosen to work there as a barber, some of the women that came in on a transport from my town of Czestochowa, I knew a lot of them. I knew them; I lived with them in my town. I lived with them in my street, and some of them were my close friends. And when they saw me, they started asking me, Abe this and Abe that—"What's going to happen to us?" What could you tell them? What could you tell?

A friend of mine worked as a barber—he was a good barber in my hometown—when his wife and his sister came into the gas chamber. . . . I can't. It's too horrible. Please.

We have to do it. You know it.

I won't be able to do it.

You have to do it. I know it's very hard. I know and I apologize.

Don't make me go on please.

Please. We must go on.

I told you today it's going to be very hard. They were taking that in bags and transporting it to Germany.

Okay, go ahead. What was his answer when his wife and sister came?

They tried to talk to him and the husband of his sister. They could not tell them this was the last time they stay alive, because behind them was the German Nazis, SS men, and they knew that if they said a word, not only the wife and the woman, who were dead already, but also they would share the same thing with them. In a way, they tried to do the best for them, with a second longer, a minute longer, just to hug them and kiss them, because they knew they would never see them again.

Franz Suchomel

In the "funnel," the women had to wait. They heard the
motors of the gas chambers. Maybe they also heard people
screaming and imploring. As they waited, "death panic"
overwhelmed them. "Death panic" makes people let go.
They empty themselves, from the front or the rear. So often,
where the women stood, there were five or six rows of excrement.

They stood?

They could squat or do it standing. I didn't see them do it, I
only saw the feces.

Only women?

Not the men, only the women. The men were chased through
the "funnel." The women had to wait until a gas chamber was
empty.

And the men?

No, they were whipped in first. You understand? They always
went first.

They didn't have to wait?

They weren't given time to wait, no.

And this "death panic"?

When this "death panic" sets in, one lets go. It's well known
when someone's terrified, and knows he's about to die; it can

happen in bed. My mother was kneeling by her bed . . .

Your mother?

Yes. Then there was a big pile. That's a fact. It's been medically proved.

Since you wanted to know: as soon as they were unloaded, if they'd been loaded in Warsaw, or elsewhere, they'd already been beaten. Beaten hard, worse than in Treblinka, I can assure you. Then during the train journey, standing in the cars, no toilets, nothing, hardly any water—fear. Then the doors opened and it started again,

"Bremze, bremze!" "Czipsze, czipsze!"

I can't pronounce it, I have false teeth. It's Polish: *Bremze* or *czipsze*.

What does bremze *mean?*

It's a Ukrainian word. It means "faster." Again the chase. A hail of whiplashes. The SS man Küttner's whip was this long. Women to the left, men to the right. And always more blows. No respite. Go in there, strip. Hurry, hurry! Always running.

Running and screaming.

That's how they were finished off.

That was the technique?

Yes, the technique. You must remember, it had to go fast. And the Blue Squad also had the task of leading the sick and the aged to the "infirmary," so as not to delay the flow of people to the gas chambers. Old people would have slowed it down. Assignment to the "infirmary" was decided by Germans. The Jews of the Blue Squad only implemented the decision, leading the people there, or carrying them on stretchers. Old women, sick children, children whose mother was sick, or whose grandmother was very old, were sent along with the grandma, because she didn't know about the "infirmary." It had a white flag with a red cross. A passage led to it. Until they reached the end, they saw nothing. Then they'd see the dead in the pit. They were forced to strip, to sit on a sandbank, and were killed with a shot in the neck. They fell into the pit. There was always a fire in the pit. With rubbish, paper and gasoline, people burn very well.

Richard Glazar

The "infirmary" was a narrow site, very close to the ramp, to which the aged were led. I had to do this too. This execution site wasn't covered, just an open place with no roof, but screened by a fence so no one could see in. The way in was a narrow passage, very short, but somewhat similar to the "funnel." A sort of tiny labyrinth. In the middle of it was a pit, and to the left as one came in, there was a little booth with a kind of wooden plank in it, like a springboard. If people were too weak to stand on it, they'd have to sit on it, and then, as the saying went in Treblinka jargon, SS man Miete would "cure each one with a single pill": a shot in the neck. In the peak periods that happened daily. In those days the pit—and it was at least ten to twelve feet deep—was full of corpses.

There were also cases of children who for some reason arrived alone, or got separated from their parents. These children were led to the "infirmary" and shot there. The "infirmary" was also for us, the Treblinka slaves, the last stop. Not the gas chamber. We always ended up in the "infirmary."

A U S C H W I T Z

Rudolf Vrba

There was always an amount of people who could not get out of the railroad cars, those who also died on the road, or people who were sick to such a degree that even persuasion with violent beating wouldn't get them moving fast enough. Those people remained in the wagons. So our first job was to get into the wagons, get out the dead bodies—or the dying—and transport them in *laufschritt,* as the Germans liked to say. This means "running." *Laufschritt,* yeah, never walking—everything had to be done in *laufschritt, immer laufen.* So, very sporty—they are a sporty nation, you see.

We have to get out those bodies, and on the ramp, running, to get them on a truck which was at the head of the ramp. There were already trucks prepared; the trucks were ready. Say, five, six, sometimes ten standing there—there was no iron rule. The first truck was for the dead and the dying. There was not much medical counting to see who is dead and who feigns to be dead, who is only simulating. So they were put on the trucks; and once this was finished, this was the first truck to move off, and it went straight to the crematorium, which was about two kilometers to the left from the ramp.

At the time it was two kilometers? Before the construction of the new ramp?

It was before the construction of the new ramp. This was the old ramp. Through the old ramp, the first one, three quarters of a million people died. This was the old ramp. I mean the majority. The new ramp was only built for the expected murder in a very short time of a million Jews from Hungary.

The whole murder machinery could work on one principle: that the people came to Auschwitz and didn't know where they were going and for what purpose. The new arrivals were supposed to be kept orderly and without panic marching into the gas chambers. Especially the panic was dangerous from women with small children. So it was important for the Nazis that none of us give some sort of message which could cause a panic, even in the last moment. And anybody who tried to get into touch with newcomers was either clubbed to death or taken behind the wagon and shot, because if a panic would have broken out, a massacre would have taken place on the spot, on the ramp. It would already be a hitch in the machinery. You can't bring in the next transport with dead bodies and blood around, because this would only increase the panic. The Nazis were concentrating on one thing: it should go in an orderly fashion so that it goes unimpeded. One doesn't lose time.

Filip Müller

Before each gassing operation the SS took stern precautions. The crematorium was ringed with SS men. Many SS men patrolled the court with dogs and machine guns. To the right were the steps that led underground to the "undressing room." In Birkenau there were four crematoriums, Crematoriums 2 and 3, and 4 and 5. Crematorium 2 was similar to 3. In 2 and 3 the "undressing room" and the gas chamber were underground. A large "undressing room" of about three thousand square feet, and a large gas chamber where one could gas up to three thousand people at a time. Crematoriums 4 and 5 were of a different type in that they weren't located underground. Everything was at ground level. In 4 and 5 there were three gas chambers, with a total capacity of at most eighteen hundred to two thousand people at a time.

As people reached the crematorium, they saw everything—this horribly violent scene. The whole area was ringed with SS. Dogs barked. Machine guns. They all, mainly the Polish Jews, had misgivings. They knew something was seriously amiss, but none of them had the faintest of notions that in three or four hours they'd be reduced to ashes.

When they reached the "undressing room," they saw that it looked like an International Information Center! On the walls were hooks, and each hook had a number. Beneath the hooks were wooden benches. So people could undress "more comfortably," it was said. And on the numerous pillars that held up this underground "undressing room," there were signs with slogans in several languages: "Clean is good!" "Lice can kill!" "Wash yourself!" "To the disinfection area." All those signs were only there to lure people into the gas chambers already undressed. And to the left, at a right angle, was the gas chamber with its massive door.

In Crematoriums 2 and 3, Zyklon gas crystals were poured in by a so-called SS disinfection squad through the ceiling, and in Crematoriums 4 and 5 through side openings. With five or six canisters of gas they could kill around two thousand people. This so-called disinfection squad arrived in a truck marked with a red cross and escorted people along to make them believe they were being led to take a bath. But the red cross was only a mask to hide the canisters of Zyklon gas and the hammers to open them. The gas took about ten to fifteen minutes to kill. The most horrible thing was when the doors of the gas chambers were opened—the unbearable sight: people were packed together like basalt, like blocks of stone. How they tumbled out of the gas chamber! I saw that several times.

That was the toughest thing to take. You could never get used to that. It was impossible.

You see, once the gas was poured in, it worked like this: it rose from the ground upwards. And in the terrible struggle that followed—because it was a struggle—the lights were switched off in the gas chambers. It was dark, no one could see, so the strongest people tried to climb higher. Because they probably realized that the higher they got, the more air there was. They could breathe better. That caused the struggle. Secondly, most people tried to push their way to the door. It was psychological: they knew where the door was; maybe they could force their way out. It was instinctive, a death struggle. Which is why children and weaker people, and the aged, always wound up at the bottom. The strongest were on top. Because in the death struggle, a father didn't realize his son lay beneath him.

And when the doors were opened?

They fell out. People fell out like blocks of stone, like rocks falling out of a truck. But near the Zyklon gas, there was a void. There was no one where the gas crystals went in. An empty space. Probably the victims realized that the gas worked strongest there. The people were battered. They struggled and fought in the darkness. They were covered in excrement, in blood, from ears and noses. One also sometimes saw that the people lying on the ground, because of the pressure of the others, were unrecognizable. Children had their skulls crushed. It was awful. Vomit. Blood—from the ears and noses, probably even menstrual fluid. I'm sure of it. There was everything in that struggle for life, that death struggle. It was terrible to see. That was the toughest part.

It was pointless to tell the truth to anyone who crossed the threshold of the crematorium. You couldn't save anyone there.

It was impossible to save people. One day in 1943 when I was already in Crematorium 5, a train from Bialystok arrived. A prisoner on the "special detail" saw a woman in the "undressing room" who was the wife of a friend of his. He came right out and told her: "You are going to be exterminated. In three hours you'll be ashes." The woman believed him because she knew him. She ran all over and warned the other women. "We're going to be killed. We're going to be gassed." Mothers carrying their children on their shoulders didn't want to hear that. They decided the woman was crazy. They chased her away. So she went to the men. To no avail. Not that they didn't believe her: they'd heard rumors in the Bialystok ghetto, or in Grodno, and elsewhere. But who wanted to hear that! When she saw that no one would listen, she scratched her whole face. Out of despair. In shock. And she started to scream.

So what happened? Everyone was gassed. The woman was held back. We had to line up in front of the ovens. First, they tortured her horribly because she wouldn't betray him. In the end she pointed to him. He was taken out of the line and thrown alive into the oven. We were told: "Whoever tells anything will end like that."

We in the special detail kept trying to figure out if there was a way we could tell people, to inform them. But our experience, in several instances where we were able to tell people, showed that it was of no use, that it made their last moments even harder to bear. At most, we thought it might help Jews from Poland, or Jews from Theresienstadt (the Czech family camp), who'd already spent six months in Birkenau. We thought it might have been of use in such cases to tell people. But imagine what it was like in other cases: Jews from Greece, from Hungary, from Corfu, who'd been traveling for ten or twelve days, starving, without water for days, dying of thirst; they were half crazed when they arrived. They were dealt with differently. They were only told: "Get undressed, you'll soon get a mug of tea." These people were in such a state, because they'd been traveling so long, that their only thought was to quench their thirst. And the SS executioners knew that very well. It was all preprogrammed, a calculated part of the extermination process, that if people were so weak, and weren't given something to drink, they'd rush into the gas chambers. But in fact, these people were already being exterminated before reaching the gas chambers. Think of the children. They begged their mothers, screaming: "Mother, please, water, water!" The adults too, who'd spent days without water, had the same obsession. Informing those people was quite pointless.

A survivor of Auschwitz (Corfu)

These are my nephews. They burned them in Birkenau too. Two of my brother's kids. They took them to the crematorium with their mom. They were all burned in Birkenau. My brother, he was sick, and they put him in the oven, in the crematorium, and burned him. That was at Birkenau.

Moshe Mordo

The oldest boy was seventeen, the second was fifteen. Two more kids *kaput* with their mom. Yes, four children I lost . . . My Dad, him too. He was eighty-five years old.

And he died in Auschwitz?

Auschwitz, that's right. Eighty-five and he died at Birkenau. My father.

Your father made the whole trip?

Yes, the whole family died. First the gas chamber, then the crematorium.

Armando Aaron, president of the Jewish community of Corfu, with four other Jewish survivors of Corfu

On Friday morning, June 9, 1944, members of the Corfu Jewish community came, very frightened, and reported to the

Germans. This square was full of Gestapo men and police, and we went forward. There were even traitors, the Recanati brothers, Athens Jews. After the war they were sentenced to life imprisonment. But they're already free. We were ordered to go forward.

How many of you were there?

Exactly 1,650. A lot of people. Christians stopped there. Christians, that's right. And they saw.

Where were the Christians?

At the street corner. Yes. And on the balconies. After we gathered here, Gestapo men with machine guns came up behind us. It was six o'clock in the morning. The day was fine.

Sixteen hundred—that's a lot of people in the street.

People gathered. The Christians heard the Jews were being rounded up, so they came.

Why'd they come?

To see the show. Let's hope it never happens again.

Were you scared?

Very scared, when we saw . . . There were young people, sick people, little children, the old, the crazy, and so on. When we saw they'd even brought the insane, even the sick from the hospital, we were frightened for the survival of the whole community.

What were you told?

That we were to appear here at the fort to be taken to work in Germany. No, Poland.

The Germans had put up a proclamation on all the walls in Corfu. It said all Jews had to report. And now that we were all rounded up, life would be better without us in Greece. It was signed by the police chiefs, by officials and by the mayors.

That it's better without Jews?

Yes. We found out after we came back, didn't we?

Was Corfu anti-Semitic? Had Corfu always had anti-Semitism?

It existed, sure, but it wasn't so strong in the years just before that. They didn't think like that against the Jews.

And now?

Now we're free.

How do you get on with the Christians now?

Very well.

What'd he say?

He asked me what you said. He agrees our relations with the Christians are very good.

Did all the Jews live in the ghetto?

Most of them.

What happened after the Jews left?

They took all our possessions, all the gold we had with us. They took the keys to our houses and stole everything.

To whom was all this given? Who stole it all?

By law, it was to go to the Greek government. But the state got only a small part of it. The rest was stolen, usurped.

By whom?

By everybody, and by the Germans. Of the 1,700 people deported, around 122 were saved. Ninety-five percent of them died.

Was it a long trip from Corfu to Auschwitz?

We were arrested here on June 9, and we finally arrived June 29. Most were burned on the night of the twenty-ninth. We stayed here for around five days. Here in the fort. No one dared escape and leave his father, mother, brothers. Our solidarity was on religious and family grounds. The first group left on June 11. I went with the second convoy on June 15.

What kind of a boat were you on?

A *zattera.* That's a boat made of barrels and planks. It was towed by a small boat with Germans in it. On our boat there were one, two or three guards, not many Germans, but we were terrified. You can understand, terror is the best of guards.

What was the journey like?

Terrible! Terrible! No water, nothing to eat, ninety in cars that were good for only twenty animals, all of us standing up.

A lot of us died. Later they put the dead in another car, in
quicklime. They burned them in Auschwitz too.

||||||||||||||||||||||||||||||||||||||||||||||||||||||||||||||||||||||||||||||||||||||||||||||||||||||||||||||||||||||||||||||||||||||||||||||||||||||||||||||||||||||||||||

**Walter Stier, ex-member of the Nazi Party, former
head of Reich Railways Department 33 of the Nazi
Party**

You never saw a train?

No, never. We had so much work, I never left my desk. We
worked day and night.

"G.E.D.O.B."

"Gedob" means . . . "Head Office of Eastbound Traffic." In
January 1940 I was assigned to Gedob Krakow. In mid-1943
I was moved to Warsaw. I was made chief traffic planner. Chief
of the Traffic Planning Office.

But your duties were the same before and after 1943?

The only change was that I was promoted to head of the
department.

What were your specific duties at Gedob in Poland during the war?

The work was barely different from the work in Germany: preparing timetables, coordinating the movement of special trains with regular trains.

There were several departments?

Yes. Department 33 was in charge of special trains . . . and regular trains. The special trains were handled by Department 33.

You were always in the department of special trains?

Yes.

What's the difference between a special and a regular train?

A regular train may be used by anyone who purchases a ticket. Say from Krakow to Warsaw. Or from Krakow to Lemberg. A special train has to be ordered. The train is specially put together and people pay group fares.

Are there still special trains now?

Of course. Just as there were then.

For group vacations you can organize a special train?

Yes, for instance, for immigrant workers returning home for the holidays special trains are scheduled. Or else one couldn't handle the traffic.

You said after the war you handled trains for visiting dignitaries.

After the war, yes.

If a king visits Germany by train that's a special train?

That's a special train. But the procedure isn't the same as for special trains for group tours, and so on. State visits are handled by the Foreign Service.

Right, but why were there more special trains during the war than before or after?

I see what you're getting at. You're referring to the so-called resettlement trains.

"Resettlement." That's it.

That's what they were called. Those trains were ordered by the Ministry of Transport of the Reich. You needed an order from the Ministry.

In Berlin?

Correct. And as for the implementation of those orders, the Head Office of Eastbound Traffic in Berlin dealt with it.

Yes, I understand.

Is that clear?

Perfectly. But mostly, at that time, who was being "resettled"?

No! We didn't know that. Only when we were fleeing from Warsaw ourselves, did we learn that they could have been Jews, or criminals, or similar people.

Jews, criminals?

Criminals. All kinds.

Special trains for criminals?

No, that was just an expression. You couldn't talk about that. Unless you were tired of life, it was best not to mention that.

But you knew that the trains to Treblinka or Auschwitz were—

Of course we knew. I was the last district; without me these trains couldn't reach their destination. For instance, a train that started in Essen had to go through the districts of Wuppertal, Hannover, Magdeburg, Berlin, Frankfurt/Oder, Posen, Warsaw, etcetera. So I had to . . .

Did you know that Treblinka meant extermination?

Of course not!

You didn't know?

Good God, no! How could we know? I never went to Treblinka. I stayed in Krakow, in Warsaw, glued to my desk.

You were a . . .

I was strictly a bureaucrat!

I see. But it's astonishing that people in the department of special trains never knew about the "final solution."

We were at war.

Because there were others who worked for the railroads who knew. Like the train conductors.

Yes, they saw it. They did. But as to what happened, I didn't . . .

What was Treblinka for you? Treblinka or Auschwitz?

Yes, for us Treblinka, Belzec and all that were concentration camps.

A destination.

Yes, that's all.

But not death.

No, no. People were put up there. For instance, for a train coming from Essen, or Cologne, or elsewhere, room had to be made for them there. With the war, and the allies advancing everywhere, those people had to be concentrated in camps.

When exactly did you find out?

Well, when the word got around, when it was whispered. It was never said outright. Good God, no! They'd have hauled you off at once! We heard things.

Rumors?

That's it, rumors.

During the war?

Toward the end of the war.

Not in 1942?

No! Good God, no! Not a word! Toward the end of 1944, maybe.

End of 1944?

Not before.

What did you . . . ?

It was said that people were being sent to concentration camps and that those in poor health probably wouldn't survive.

Extermination came to you as a big surprise?

Completely. Yes.

You had no idea.

Not the slightest. Like that camp—what was its name? It was in the Oppeln district . . . I've got it: Auschwitz!

Yes. Auschwitz was in the Oppeln district.

Right. Auschwitz wasn't far from Krakow.

That's true.

We never heard a word about that.

Auschwitz to Krakow is forty miles.

That's not very far. And we knew nothing. Not a clue.

But you knew that the Nazis—that Hitler didn't like the Jews.

That we did. It was well known; it appeared in print. It was
no secret. But as to their extermination, that was news to us.
I mean, even today people deny it. They say there couldn't
have been so many Jews. Is it true? I don't know. That's what
they say. Anyway, what was done was an outrage, to put it
bluntly.

What?

The extermination. Everyone condemns it. Every decent person. But as for knowing about it, we didn't.

But the Polish people, for instance, knew everything.

That's not surprising. They lived nearby, they heard, they
talked. And they didn't have to keep quiet.

Raul Hilberg

This is the *Fahrplananordnung 587*, which is typical for special
trains. The number of the order goes to show you how many
of them there were. Underneath: *Nur für den Dienstgebrauch*—
"Only for internal use." But this turns out to be a very low
classification for secrecy. And the fact that in this entire docu-

ment, which after all deals with death trains, one cannot see—
not only on this one, one cannot see it on others—the word
geheim, "secret," is astonishing to me. That they would not
have done that is very astonishing. On second thought, I believe that had they labeled it secret, they would have invited
a great many inquiries from people who got hold of it. They
would then perhaps have raised more questions; they would
have focused attention on the thing. And the key to the entire

operation from the psychological standpoint was never to utter
the words that would be appropriate to the action being taken.
Say nothing; do these things; do not describe them. So therefore this *"Nur für den Dienstgebrauch."* And now notice to how
many recipients this particular order goes. "Bfe"—*Bahnhofe.*
On this stretch there are one, two, three, four, five, six, seven,
eight, and here we are in Malkinia, which is of course the
station near Treblinka. But notice that it takes eight recipients

for this relatively short distance through Radom to the Warsaw district—eight, because the train passes through these stations. Therefore, each one has to know. Not only that, but of course you're not going to write two pieces of paper if you can write only one. Therefore, we find here not only PKR, which is a death train, going here in the plan labeled thus, but we also see the empty train after it has arrived in Treblinka, now originating in Treblinka, and you can always know whether it's an empty train with the letter *L* in front of it, *leer*, and now—

Ruckleitung des Leerzuges, *which means "return of the empty train."*

—the train returns empty. And now we're going back. Then we have another train. Now notice that there is very little subtlety to this numbering system. We are going from 9228 to 9229, to 9230, to 9231, to 9232. Hardly any originality here. It's just very regular traffic.

Death traffic.

Death traffic. And here we see that starting out in one ghetto, which obviously is being emptied, the train leaves for Treblinka. It leaves on the thirtieth of September, 1942, eighteen minutes after four o'clock—by the schedule at least—and arrives there at eleven twenty-four on the next morning. This is also a very long train, which may be the reason it is so slow. It's a 50G—*fünfzig Güterwagen*—fifty freight cars filled with people. That's an exceptionally heavy transport. Now once the train has been unloaded at Treblinka—and you notice there are two numbers here: 11:24, that's in the morning, and 15:59, which is to say almost four o'clock in the afternoon—in that interval of time the train has to be unloaded, cleaned and turned around. And you see here the same numbers appear as the *Leerzug,* the now empty train, goes to another place. And it leaves at four o'clock in the afternoon and goes now to that other place which is yet another small town where it picks up victims. And there you are at three o'clock in the morning. It leaves on the twenty-third at three o'clock in the morning. And arrives there the next day.

What is that? It seems to be the same train.

It is the same—quite obviously the same. The number has to be changed quite obviously. Correct. Then it goes back to Treblinka and this is again a long trip; and it now goes back to yet another place—the same situation, the same trip. And then yet another. Goes to Treblinka and then arrives in Czesto-chowa the twenty-ninth of September and then the cycle is complete. And this is called a *Fahrplananordnung.* If you count up the number of not empty trains but full ones—PKRs—there's one—there's one here, that's two, that's three, that's four—we may be talking about ten thousand dead Jews on this one *Fahrplananordnung* here.

More than ten thousand.

Well, we will be conservative here.

But why is this document so fascinating, as a matter of fact? Because I was in Treblinka, and to have the two things to-gether . . .

Well, you see, when I hold a document in my hand, particu-larly if it's an original document, then I hold something which is actually something that the original bureaucrat held in his hand. It's an artifact. It's a leftover. It's the only leftover there is. The dead are not around. The Reichsbahn was ready to ship in principle any cargo in return for payment. And therefore, the basic key—price-controlled key—was that Jews were going to be shipped to Treblinka, were going to be shipped to Auschwitz, Sobibor or any other destination so long as the railroads were paid by the track kilometer, so many pfennigs per mile. The rate was the same throughout the war. With children under ten going at half-fare and children under four going free. Payment had to be made for only one way. The guards, of course, had to have return fare paid for them because they were going back to their place of origin.

Excuse me, the children under four who were shipped to the extermination camps, the children under four . . .

. . . went free.

They had the privilege to be gassed freely?

Yes, transport was free. In addition to that, because the person who had to pay, the agency that had to pay, was the agency that ordered the train—and that happened to have been the Gestapo, Eichmann's office—because of the financial problem which that office had in making payment, the Reichsbahn agreed on group fares. The Jews were being shipped in much the same way that any excursion group would be granted a special fare if there were enough people traveling. The minimum was four hundred, a kind of charter fare. Four hundred minimum. So even if there were fewer than four hundred, it would pay to say there were four hundred and in that way get the half-fare for adults as well. And that was the basic principle. Now of course if there were exceptional filth in the cars, which might be the case, if there was damage to the equipment, which might be the case because the transports took so long and because five to ten percent of the prisoners died en route. Then there might be an additional bill for that damage. But in principle, so long as payment was being made, transports were being shipped. Sometimes the SS got credit. Sometimes the transport went out before payment, because as you see, the whole business was handled as in the case of any other charter traffic especially or any really personal traffic of any kind through a travel bureau. Mittel Europäisch Reisebüro (The Middle Europe Travel Agency) would handle some of these transactions—the billing procedure, the ticketing procedure—or if a smaller transport was involved, the SS would . . .

It was the same bureau that was dealing with any kind of normal passenger?

Absolutely. Just the official travel bureau. Mittel Europäisch Reisebüro would ship people to the gas chambers or they will ship vacationers to their favorite resort, and that was basically the same office and the same operation, the same procedure, the same billing.

No difference?

No difference whatsoever. As a matter of course, everybody would do that job as if it were the most normal thing to do.

It was not a normal job.

No, it was not a normal job. As a matter of fact, you know, even the complicated currency procedures were followed in much the same way as with any other transactions if borders had to be crossed, and that was very frequent. I think the most interesting example is of course Greece, the transports from Salonika, Greece, in the spring of 1943, involving some forty-

six thousand victims over a considerable distance, so that even
with group fare the bill came to almost 2 million marks, which
was quite a sum. And the basic principle, you see, with such
traffic is that which is employed in the customary way, even
to this day, all over the world. One pays in the currency of the
place of origin, but then one has to pay the participating railroads en route in their own currencies.

From Salonika they had to cross Greece—it was drachmas.

In Greece it was drachmas, and then you might have to go
through the Serbian and Croatian railroads, and you might
then have to go to the Reichsbahn and pay in marks. Now
ironically, the problem was, you see, that the military commander in Salonika who was in charge—so he in a sense was the
ultimate person responsible for paying for these things—didn't
have the marks, though he did have the drachmas, you see,
from the confiscated Jewish property which was used to pay
for these things. This was a self-financing principle. The SS or
the military would confiscate Jewish property and with the
proceeds, especially from bank deposits, would pay for transports.

You mean that the Jews themselves had to pay for their death?

You have to remember one basic principle. There was no
budget for destruction. So that is the reason confiscated property had to be used in order to make the payments. All right.
The property of the Jews in Salonika was confiscated, but the
proceeds were in local Greek currency. The Reichsbahn, of
course, would want payment in marks. How then do you
change the drachmas into marks? Now you have exchange
controls, right within occupied Europe. The only way it could
be done, of course, is if somebody in this occupied zone ob-

tained marks. But how could they? This was not such a simple thing in wartime, and therefore for once there was a default, and the railroad shipped all of these Jews to Auschwitz without compensation.

‖‖

A U S C H W I T Z

Filip Müller

The life of the "special detail" depended on the trainloads due for extermination. When a lot of them came in, the "special detail" was enlarged. They couldn't do without the detail, so there was no weeding out. But when there were fewer trainloads, it meant immediate extermination for us. We in the "special detail" knew that a lack of trains would lead to our liquidation.

The "special detail" lived in a crisis situation. Every day we saw thousands and thousands of innocent people disappear up the chimney. With our own eyes, we could truly fathom what it means to be a human being. There they came, men, women, children, all innocent. They suddenly vanished, and the world said nothing! We felt abandoned. By the world, by humanity. But the situation taught us fully what the possibility of survival meant. For we could gauge the infinite value of human life. And we were convinced that hope lingers in man as long as he lives. Where there's life, hope must never be relinquished. That's why we struggled through our lives of hardship, day after day, week after week, month after month, year after year, hoping against hope to survive, to escape that hell.

T R E B L I N K A

Franz Suchomel

At that time, in, say, January, February, March, hardly any trains arrived.

Was Treblinka glum without the trains?

I wouldn't say the Jews were glum. They became so when they realized . . . I'll come to that later; it's a story in itself. The Jews, those in the work squads, thought at first that they'd survive. But in January, when they stopped receiving food, for Wirth had decreed that there were too many of them . . . There were a good five to six hundred of them in Camp 1.

Up there?

Yes. To keep them from rebelling, they weren't shot or gassed, but starved. Then an epidemic broke out, a kind of typhus. The Jews stopped believing they'd make it. They were left to die. They dropped like flies. It was all over. They'd stopped believing. It was all very well to say . . . I . . . we kept on insisting: "You're going to live!" We almost believed it ourselves. If you lie enough, you believe your own lies. Yes. But they replied to me: "No, chief, we're just reprieved corpses."

Richard Glazar

The "dead season," as it was called, began in February 1943, after the big trainloads came in from Grodno and Bialystok. Absolute quiet. It quieted in late January, February and into March. Nothing. Not one trainload. The whole camp was empty, and suddenly, everywhere, there was hunger. It kept increasing. And one day when the famine was at its peak, Obersharführer Kurt Franz appeared before us and told us: "The trains will be coming in again starting tomorrow." We didn't say anything. We just looked at each other, and each of us thought: "Tomorrow the hunger will end." In that period we were actively planning the rebellion. We all wanted to survive until the rebellion.

The trainloads came from an assembly camp in Salonika. They'd brought in Jews from Bulgaria, Macedonia. These were rich people; the passenger cars bulged with possessions. Then an awful feeling gripped us, all of us, my companions as well as myself, a feeling of helplessness, of shame. For we threw ourselves on their food. A detail brought a crate full of crackers, another full of jam. They deliberately dropped the crates, falling over each other, filling their mouths with crackers and jam. The trainloads from the Balkans brought us to a terrible realization: we were the workers in the Treblinka factory, and our lives depended on the whole manufacturing process, that is, the slaughtering process at Treblinka.

This realization came suddenly with the fresh trainloads?

Maybe it wasn't so sudden, but it was only with the Balkan trainloads that it became so stark to us, unadorned.

Why?

Twenty-four thousand people, probably with not a sick person among them, not an invalid, all healthy and robust! I recall our watching them from our barracks. They were already naked, milling among their baggage. And David—David Bratt—said to me: "Maccabees! The Maccabees have arrived in Treblinka!" Sturdy, physically strong people, unlike the others.

Fighters?

Yes, they could have been fighters. It was staggering for us, for these men and women, all splendid, were wholly unaware of what was in store for them. Wholly unaware. Never before had things gone so smoothly and quickly. Never. We felt ashamed, and also that this couldn't go on, that something had to happen. Not just a few people acting, but all of us.

The idea was almost ripe back in November 1942. Beginning in November '42, we'd noticed . . . that we were being "spared," in quotes. We noticed it and we also learned that Stangl, the commandant, wanted, for efficiency's sake, to hang on to men who were already trained specialists in the various jobs: sorters, corpse haulers, barbers who cut the women's hair, and so on. This in fact is what later gave us the chance to prepare, to organize the uprising. We had a plan worked out in January 1943, code-named "The Time." At a set time we were to attack the SS everywhere, seize their weapons and attack the *Kommandantur*. But we couldn't do it because things were at a standstill in the camp, and because typhus had already broken out.

‖‖‖

AUSCHWITZ

Filip Müller

In the fall of 1943, when it was clear to all of us that no one would help us unless we helped ourselves, a key question faced us all: for us in the "special detail," was there any chance to halt this wave of extermination and still save our lives? We could see only one: armed rebellion. We thought that if we could get hold of a few weapons and secure the participation of all the inmates throughout the camp, there was a chance of success. That was the essential thing. That's why our liaison men contacted the leaders of the Resistance movement, first in Birkenau, then in Auschwitz 1, so the revolt could be coordinated everywhere. The answer came that the Resistance command in Auschwitz 1 agreed with our plan and would join with us. Unfortunately, among the Resistance leaders there were very few Jews. Most were political prisoners whose lives weren't at stake, and for whom each day of life lived through increased their chances of survival. For us in the "special detail," it was the opposite.

Rudolf Vrba

Auschwitz-Birkenau was far from being only a mass murder center. It was a normal concentration camp too, which had its order, like Mauthausen, like Buchenwald, like Dachau, like Sachsenhausen. But whereas in Mauthausen the main product of prisoners' work was stone—there was a big stone quarry— the product in Auschwitz was death. Everything was geared to keep the crematorium running. This was the aim. This meant the prisoners would work on the road to the crematorium, would build the crematorium. They would build all barracks necessary for keeping up prisoners, and of course, apart from that, there was an element of a normal German concentration camp—the Krupp and Siemens factories moved in and utilized slave labor. So the Krupp factory and the Siemens factory were built partly within the concentration camp Auschwitz-Birkenau.

The tradition in the concentration camp was that there was a considerable amount of political prisoners, trade unionists, social democrats, communists, ex-fighters from Spain. What happened was a very peculiar development. The Resistance leadership in Auschwitz was concentrated in the hands of German-speaking anti-Nazis who were German by birth but considered racially pure by the Nazi hierarchy. They got a bit better treatment than the rest of the camp. I don't say they were treated with gloves, but they managed with time to gain influence over various Nazi dignitaries from the SS and to use it in a way which led systematically to an improvement of conditions within the concentration camp itself. Whereas in 1943 . . . 1942, in Birkenau, in December and January a death rate of four hundred prisoners per day was common, by May 1943, not only because of the weather improvement but due to the activities of the Resistance movement, the improvement was so marked that the mortality rate greatly decreased in the concentration camp. And they considered it a great victory on their side.

And that improvement of living conditions within the con-centration camp was perhaps not so against the policy of the higher echelons of SS ranks as long as it did not interfere with the objective of the camp, which was production of death on the newcomers who were not prisoners of the camp. There was a rule that those people in the transport who can be utilized for work, who are in good physical condition—they are not old, they are not too young, they are not children, they are not women with children, etcetera, etcetera, they look healthy—they should come into the concentration camp for replacement of those who were dying in the concentration camp, as a fresh force. And I would see—the following discussion I once overheard: A transport came from—I think it was from Holland or from Belgium, I do not guarantee you which one it was—and the SS doctor selected a group of well-looking Jewish prisoners, newcomers, from the whole transport which would be gassed, which was gassed. The representative of the SS from the concentration camp says he doesn't want them. And there was a discussion between them which I could overhear in which the doctor was saying: "Why don't you take them, they are *ausgefressen Juden auf holländisch Käse.*" This means "Jews full of, well nourished on Dutch cheese." He said they would be good for the camp. And Fries it was—Hauptscharführer Fries said: "I can't take them, because nowadays they don't kick the bucket so fast in the camp."

This means they don't die fast enough?

That's right. In other words, he explained that if the needs of the camp were, say, thirty thousand prisoners, and five thousand died, they were replaced by a new force from the Jewish transport which came in. But if only a thousand died, well, only a thousand were replaced and more went into the gas chamber. So the improvement of the conditions within the concentration camp itself made a higher death rate in the gas chamber, straight into the gas chamber. It decreased the death rate among the prisoners in the concentration camp. So here it was clear to me that the improvement of the situation in the concentration camp does not impede the process of mass executions of those people who are brought into the camp. Consequently, my idea then of the Resistance movement, of the sense of the Resistance movement, was that the improvement of the conditions within the camp is only a first step, that the main thing is to stop the process of mass execution, the machinery of the killing, and that therefore it is a time of preparation, of gathering forces for attacking the SS from inside—even if it is a suicide mission—but destroying the machinery. And in this respect I would consider it as a suitable objective, worthy objective, and it was also clear to me that such an objective cannot be achieved overnight, that there is necessary a lot of preparation, and a lot of circumstances about which being only a small cog in the whole machinery of the Resistance I could not know or decide. But it was clear in my mind that the only objective of any resistance within the concentration camp of the type of Auschwitz has to be different from that in Mauthausen or Dachau. Because whereas in Mauthausen or Dachau this policy of resistance improved the survival rate of political prisoners, the same very noble policy improved and oiled the machinery of mass annihilation as practiced by the Nazis within the Auschwitz camp.

AUSCHWITZ

Ruth Elias (Israel), deported from Theresienstadt, survivor of Auschwitz

In Theresienstadt, this time in which passed transport to the east, we were loaded into these wagons for cattle, and it went for two days and one night. The second day, it was December, but it was warm inside, because we made the heat, we heated it up with our temperature, body temperature. One

evening the train came to a stop. The next day in the evening the doors were opened and there was a terrible screaming: "Out, out, out, out!" We were shocked, we didn't know what was going on, where we are, we saw only SS with dogs, and we saw in the distance symmetric lights, but we didn't know where we are, what the lights, the thousands of lights, are meaning. We only heard the shouting: "Out, out, out!" Out! Yes, exactly. And *"Schnell, schnell, schnell."* Out we came from these wagons, and we had to line up, and there were some people with striped uniforms. We didn't know what the stripes are and I asked one in Czech: "Where are we?" and it was a Polish one who understand my Czech, and he told me Auschwitz. But it didn't mean anything to me. What is Auschwitz? I didn't know about Auschwitz anything. We were led into a so-called family camp, Familienlage B2B. Children, men and women together without any selection beforehand. Men from the *Männerlager* came in and told us that Auschwitz is a *Vernichtungslager*, an extermination camp, where they are gassing people, and we didn't believe. In this camp there was already a transport who left Theresienstadt in September, three months before us. They didn't believe too, because we were all together and nobody was taken away, nobody was burnt. We didn't believe it.

Rudolf Vrba

These Czech Jews from Theresienstadt, from the ghetto near Prague, came into one particular part of the camp which was called Bauabschnitt 2B. At that time I was working as a registrar in 2A. The division between 2A and 2B was only one electrical fence through which nobody could climb, but you could speak through it. In the morning I could sort out the whole situation. There were a number of surprising circumstances. The families—which means men, women and children—were taken together, and nobody was gassed. They took with them their luggage into the camp and they were not shorn—their hair was left.

So they were in a different position from anything that I had seen until now. I didn't know what to think about it, nobody knew, but in the main registrar's office it was known that all the people have got special cards which had a remark on them: *SB mit sechs monatiger Quarantäne. SB*—we knew what that means: *Sonderbehandlung*, "special treatment," which meant gassing. And *Quarantäne* also, we knew what it means. But it didn't make sense to us that somebody should be kept in the camp for six months in order to be gassed after six months. Therefore, it was left open to interpretation if SB —*Sonderbehandlung*—always means gassing or if perhaps it has a double meaning. And the six months was supposed to end on March 7. In December—and I think it was close to December 20—another transport from Theresienstadt came, also about four thousand people strong, which was added to the first transport in the camp B2B. Also men, women and children were left together—families were not torn apart. Old people, young people, everything remained intact, and their hair was left and their personal property was left, so they could wear civilian clothes, whatever they had. They were given a sort of a different treatment. A school was arranged for the children in a special barrack and the children soon made a theater there. But it was not really a very comfortable life, because they were cramped, and from the first four thousand people during the first six months, the mortality was about a thousand.

Were they obliged to work?

Yes, they had to work, but only inside their camp. They made a new camp road and ornamented their barracks. They were induced to write letters, induced to write letters by the SS, to their relatives in the Theresienstadt ghetto, saying that they are all together, etcetera.

Were there better conditions of food?

Definitely better conditions of food, better conditions of treatment. I mean their conditions were so good that within six months—including the old people and children—only one quarter of them died. I mean this was a very unusually good condition in Auschwitz. And at the children's theater the SS used to come and play with the children. Personal relationship was struck up. And of course, one of my tasks as a registrar was to find out the possibility of people who are Resistance, who had a mind for resistance, and to strike up a relationship and contracts.

You were already a member of the Resistance movement in Auschwitz?

Yes. And that was my job as a registrar, that I had the possibility of moving a bit around on various pretexts, to carry papers from my part of the camp to the central registry and on that occasion to meet other people and give them messages, take messages from them. And one of my tasks then was—because I was closest to the camp—to find out if among the members of this transport were people suitable for organizing a Resistance nucleus. We soon found several ex-members of the International Brigade in Spain. And so in no time I had a list of about forty people who had a record from the past of developing some kind of resistance against the Nazis. A special figure emerged in this family camp. The name was Freddy Hirsch. He was a German Jew who emigrated from Germany to Prague. Freddy Hirsch showed a considerable amount of interest for the education of the children who were there—he knew each child by name—and by his upright behavior and obvious human dignity he became a sort of spiritual leader of this whole family camp. Now March 7 started to near and this was supposed to give us the signal of what was supposed to happen. But what, we did not know for sure.

Filip Müller

At the end of February, I was in a night squad at Crematorium 5. Around midnight, there appeared a man from the political section, Oberscharführer Hustek. He handed Oberscharführer Voss a note. Voss was then in charge of the four crematoriums. I saw Voss unfold the note and talk to himself, saying: "Sure, always Voss. What'd they do without Voss? How can we do it?" That's how he talked to himself. Suddenly, he told me: "Go get the kapos." I fetched the kapos—kapo Schloime, and kapo Wacek. They came in, and he asked them: "How many pieces are left?" By "pieces" he meant bodies. They told him: "Around five hundred pieces." He said: "By morning those five hundred pieces must be reduced to ashes. You're sure it's five hundred?" "Just about," they said. "Assholes! What do you mean, 'just about'?" Then he left for the "undressing room" to see for himself—where the bodies were. They were piled there; at Crematorium 5, the "undressing room" also served as a warehouse for bodies.

After the gassing?

After the gassing the bodies were dragged there. Voss went there to check. He forgot the note, leaving it on the table. I quickly scanned it, and was shocked by what I read. The crematorium was to be gotten ready for the "special treatment" of the Czech family camp.

In the morning, when the day squad came on, I ran into kapo Kaminski, one of the Resistance leaders in the "special detail," and told him the news. He informed me that Crematorium 2 was also being prepared. That the ovens were ready there too. And he exhorted me: "You have friends and fellow countrymen. Some are locksmiths. Go see them. They're allowed to go into Camp B2B. Tell them to warn these people of what's in store for them, and say that if they defend themselves, we'll reduce the crematoriums to ashes. And at camp B2B, they can immediately burn down their barracks." We were certain that the next night these people would be gassed. But when no night squad went out, we were relieved. The deadline had been postponed for a few days. But many prisoners, including the Czechs in the family camp, accused us of spreading panic, of having circulated false reports.

Rudolf Vrba

By approximately the end of February, a rumor was spread by the Nazis that the family transport will be moved to a place called Heidebreck. The first move was to separate the first family transport from the second family transport by transferring them overnight into the quarantine camp B2A, where I was the registrar.

So I could now speak to those people directly. I talked to Freddy Hirsch specifically, and I told him about the possibility that the transport that has been his transport, the family transport of the Czechs, has been transferred to the quarantine camp because of the possibility of them being predestined to be gassed on the seventh of March. He asked me if I know that for sure, and I said I do not know it for sure, but it is a serious possibility, because there is no record of any train going away from Auschwitz, and usually the offices of the registrars, where the Resistance movement had their people, would get wind of such information, of a transport being prepared out of Auschwitz, and there was no such information. And I explained him the circumstances, and I explained him what it means, and the possibility then would arise that for the first time there in camp people who are relatively physically preserved, who have retained some sort of a morale, who are certain to go to die, in other words, to be subject to the normal execution procedure —the anonymous, major execution procedure as usual—and they will know it, they can't be just tricked, and that this is perhaps the time to act. And the action of course will have to come out from them. Because there are others whose death was imminent, and that was the people from the Sonderkommando, who work in the crematorium, which was periodically replaced. And they show the willingness that if the Czechs before the gassing attack the SS, they will join them. Freddy Hirsch objected. He was very reasonable, and he said it doesn't make sense that the Germans would keep them for six months, feeding the children with milk and white bread, in order to gas them after six months.

On the next day I got a message again from the Resistance that it is sure that they are going to be gassed, that the Sonderkommando already received the coal for burning the transport. The Sonderkommando knew exactly how many people are going to be gassed, what sort of people, because there are certain rules. So I called up again to Freddy and explained to him that as far as this transport is concerned, including him, they are going to be gassed in the next forty-eight hours. So he sadly started to worry. He asked: what happens to the children if we start the uprising. He had a very close relation with the children.

How many children were there?

There could have been a hundred, alive.

And how many people able to fight?

Well, the nucleus was about thirty, and now it was not necessary to keep any precautions, and this depends. I mean, if it comes to fighting, even an old woman can pick up a stone. Anybody can fight. I mean this is difficult to predict. But it was necessary to have a nucleus, and it was necessary to have a leading personality. You see, those are small details which are extremely important. And so he said to me: "If we make the uprising, what is going to happen to the children? Who is going to take care of them?" I said that I cannot say anything exact; that there is no way out for them. They will die whatsoever. That's for sure. This he cannot prevent. What does depend on us: who is going to die with them, and how many SS are going to die with them, and how will it impede the whole machinery, plus the possibility that a part during the uprising will find a way out of the camp, which is possible in such a situation. I mean, to break through the guards, because once the uprising starts, some weapons can be expected to be had. And I explained to him that there is absolutely no chance for him or for anybody from that transport—to the best of my knowledge, and everybody else's knowledge whom I trust— to survive the next forty-eight hours.

This took place inside the block?

Inside the block, in my room. And I told him also of the need for a personality and that he has been selected. And of course, he explains to me that he understands the situation, that it is extremely difficult for him to make any decisions because of the children, and that he cannot see how he can just leave those children to their fate. He was sort of their father. I mean he was only thirty at that time, but the relationship between him and those children was very strong. And he said to me that of course he can see the logic behind my argumentation and that he would like to think about it for an hour, if I could leave him alone to think for an hour. And because I had at that time a room of my own as a registrar, I left him in my room, which was equipped with a table, a chair, and a bed, and some writing instrumentation, and I told him I would come in an hour's time back.

And I came back in an hour, and I could see that he is laying on my bed and that he's dying. He was cyanotic in the face, he had froth around the mouth, and I could see that he has poisoned himself. He took poison. But he was not dead. And because of him being so important . . . I didn't know what sort of poison he took, but I had again a connection to a man called Dr. Kleinmann. This Dr. Kleinmann was of Polish origin and a French Jew and medically qualified, and I called him immediately to Hirsch and asked him to do what he can because this is an important man. And Kleinmann inspected Freddy Hirsch, and he says he thinks he poisoned himself with a big dose of barbiturates, that it might perhaps be possible to save his life. But he won't be on his feet for a long time to come, and he is going to be gassed in the next forty-eight hours, and he thinks, Kleinmann, that it would be better to leave things as they are and to do nothing.

Well, the story after the suicide of Freddy Hirsch developed very fast. First thing, I informed the rest of them what I had told Hirsch. Secondly, I moved to camp 2D to establish contact with the Resistance movement there. They gave me bread for the people—yes, bread and onions—and said that no decision has been made and I should come later for instructions. The moment I distributed the bread something happened, namely, a special curfew was made within the camp, all administrative activities were stopped, all guards were doubled, machine guns, etcetera, were spread around the quarantine camp, and I was out of contact. The Czech family transport was gassed in the evening. They were put on trucks. All of them knew. They were put on trucks. They behaved very well. We didn't know of course where the trucks were going. They were being assured once more that they were going to Heidebreck and not to be gassed, and we knew that if they are going out from the camp, the trucks will turn right when they leave the camp. And we knew that if they turn left there was only one way. Five hundred yards. That's where the crematorium was.

Filip Müller

That night I was at Crematorium 2. As soon as the people got out of the vans, they were blinded by floodlights and forced through a corridor to the stairs leading to the "undressing room." They were blinded, made to run. Blows were rained on them. Those who didn't run fast enough were beaten to death by the SS. The violence used against them was extraordinary. And sudden.

Without explanation?

Not a word. As soon as they left the vans, the beatings began. When they entered the "undressing room," I was standing near the rear door, and from there I witnessed the frightful scene. The people were bloodied. They knew then where they were. They stared at the pillars of the so-called International Information Center I've mentioned, and that terrified them. What they read didn't reassure them. On the contrary, it panicked them. They knew the score. They'd learned at Camp B2B what went on there. They were in despair. Children clung to each other. Their mothers, their parents, the old people all cried, overcome with misery. Suddenly, some SS officers appeared on the steps, including the camp commandant, Schwarzhuber. He'd given them his word as an SS officer that they'd be transferred to Heidebreck. So they all began to cry out, to beg, shouting: "Heidebreck was a trick! We were lied to! We want to live! We want to work!" They looked their SS executioners in the eye, but the SS men remained impassive, just staring at them. There was a movement in the crowd. They probably wanted to rush to the SS men and tell them how they'd been lied to, but then some guards surged forward, wielding clubs, and more people were injured.

In the "undressing room"?

Yes. The violence climaxed when they tried to force the people to undress. A few obeyed, only a handful. Most of them refused to follow the order. Suddenly, like a chorus, they all began to sing. The whole "undressing room" rang with the Czech national anthem, and the *Hatikvah*. That moved me terribly, that . . .

That was happening to my countrymen, and I realized that my life had become meaningless. Why go on living? For what? So I went into the gas chamber with them, resolved to die. With them. Suddenly, some who recognized me came up to me. For my locksmith friends and I had sometimes gone into the family camp. A small group of women approached. They looked at me and said, right there in the gas chamber . . .

You were inside the gas chamber?

Yes. One of them said: "So you want to die. But that's senseless. Your death won't give us back our lives. That's no way. You must get out of here alive, you must bear witness to our suffering, and to the injustice done to us."

Rudolf Vrba

That's how it ended with the first Czech family transport. And it was quite clear to me then that the Resistance in the camp is not geared for an uprising but for survival of the members of the Resistance. I then decided to act what was called by the members of the Resistance anarchic and individualistic activity, like escape and leaving the community, for which I am coresponsible by that time. The decision to escape, in spite of the policy of the Resistance movement at that time, was formed immediately, and I started to press on with the preparations for the escape together with my friend Wetzler, who was extremely important in this matter. And before I left I spoke with Hugo Lenek. Hugo Lenek was in command of the Resistance group in the second family transport. I explained to him that from the Resistance movement they can expect nothing now —expect nothing but bread. But when it comes to the dying, they should act on their own. As far as I was concerned, I think that if I successfully manage to break out from the camp and bring the information to the right place at the right time, that this might be a help, that I might manage, if I succeed, to bring help from outside. And also it was a firm belief in me that all this was possible, because either the victims who came to Auschwitz didn't know what was happening there or if somebody had the knowledge outside, that the knowledge was ... I would say that they didn't know. That's it. And I thought that if this would be made known by any means within Europe, and especially within Hungary, from where a million Jews were supposed to be transported to Auschwitz immediately, in May—and I knew about that—that this might stir up the Resistance outside and bring help from outside directly to Auschwitz. And thus the escape plans are finally formulated and the escape took place on April 7.

And this is the main and the deep reason why you decided to escape?

Suddenly, at that moment, to press on with it? In other words, not to delay anything but to escape as soon as possible. To inform the world.

About what was going on?

Right.

In Auschwitz?

Right.

W A R S A W

Jan Karski, university professor (USA), former courier of the Polish government in exile

Now . . . now I go back thirty-five years. No, I don't go back . . . I come back. I am ready.

In the middle of 1942, I was thinking to take up again my position as a courier between the Polish underground and the Polish government in exile in London. The Jewish leaders in Warsaw learned about it. A meeting was arranged, outside the ghetto. There were two gentlemen. They did not live in the ghetto. They introduced themselves—leader of Bund, Zionist leader.

Now, what transpired, what happened in our conversation? First, I was not prepared for it. I was relatively isolated in my work in Poland. I did not see many things. In thirty-five years after the war I do not go back. I have been a teacher for twenty-six years. I never mention the Jewish problem to my students. I understand this film is for historical record, so I will try to do it.

They described to me what is happening to the Jews. Did I know about it? No, I didn't. They described to me first that the Jewish problem is unprecedented, cannot be compared with the Polish problem, or Russian, or any other problem. Hitler will lose this war, but he will exterminate all the Jewish population. Do I understand it? The Allies fight for their people—they fight for humanity. The Allies cannot forget that the Jews will be exterminated totally in Poland—Polish and European Jews. They were breaking down. They paced the room. They were whispering. They were hissing. It was a nightmare for me.

Did they look completely despairing?

Yes. Yes. At various stages of the conversation they lost control of themselves. I just sat in my chair. I just listened. I did not even react. I didn't ask them questions. I was just listening.

They wanted to convince you?

They realized, I think . . . they realized from the beginning that I don't know, that I don't understand this problem. Once I said I will take messages from them, they wanted to inform me what is happening to the Jews. I didn't know this. I was never in a ghetto. I never dealt with the Jewish matters.

Did you know yourself at the time that most of the Jews of Warsaw had already been killed?

I did know. But I didn't see anything. I never heard any description of what was happening and I was never there. It is one thing to know statistics. There were hundreds of thousands of Poles also killed—of Russians, Serbs, Greeks. We knew about it. But it was a question of statistics.

Did they insist on the complete uniqueness . . . ?

Yes. This was their problem: to impress upon me—and that was my mission—to impress upon all people whom I am going to see that the Jewish situation is unprecedented in history. Egyptian pharaohs did not do it. The Babylonians did not do it. Now for the first time in history actually, they came to the conclusion: unless the Allies take some unprecedented steps, regardless of the outcome of the war, the Jews will be totally exterminated. And they cannot accept it.

This means that they asked for very specific measures?

Yes. Interchangeably. At a certain point the Bund leader, then at a certain point the Zionist leader—then what do they want? What message am I supposed to take? Then they gave me messages, various messages, to the Allied governments as such —I was to see as many government officials as I could, of course. Then to the Polish government, then to the president of the Polish republic. Then to the international Jewish leaders. And to individual political leaders, leading intellectuals—approach as many people as possible. And then they gave me segments—to whom do I report what. So now, in these nightmarish meetings—two meetings I had with them—well, then they presented their demands. Separate demands. The message was: Hitler cannot be allowed to continue extermination. Every day counts. The Allies cannot treat this war only from a purely military strategic standpoint. They will win the war if they take such an attitude, but what good will it do to us? We will not survive this war. The Allied governments cannot take such a stand. We contributed to humanity—we gave scientists for thousands of years. We originated great religions. We are humans. Do you understand it? Do you understand it? Never happened before in history, what is happening to our people now. Perhaps it will shake the conscience of the world.

We understand we have no country of our own, we have no government, we have no voice in the Allied councils. So we have to use services, little people like you are. Will you do it? Will you approach them? Will you fulfill your mission? Approach the Allied leaders? We want an official declaration of the Allied nations that in addition to the military strategy which aims at securing victory, military victory in this war, extermination of the Jews forms a separate chapter, and the Allied nations formally, publicly, announce that they will deal with this problem, that it becomes a part of their overall strategy in this war. Not only defeat of Germany but also

saving the remaining Jewish population. Once they make
such an official declaration, they have an air force, they drop
bombs on Germany—why cannot they drop millions of leaf-
lets informing the German population exactly what their
government is doing to the Jews? Perhaps they don't know
it! Now let them make an official declaration—again, official,
a public declaration—that if the German nation does not
offer evidence of trying to change the policy of their government, the German nation will have to be held responsible for
the crimes their government is committing. And now, if
there is no such evidence, to announce publicly, officially,
certain objects in Germany will be bombed, destroyed, as a
retaliation for what the German government is doing against
the Jews, that the bombing which will take place is not a part
of the military strategy. It deals only with the Jewish problem. Let the German people know before bombing takes
place and after bombing takes place that this was done and
will continue to be done because the Jews are being exterminated in Poland. Perhaps it will help. They can do it.
They can do it. This was one mission.

Next, both of them—particularly the Zionist leader—he was
again whispering, hissing. Something is going to happen. The
Jews in the Warsaw ghetto are talking about it, particularly the
young elements. They will fight. They speak about a declaration of war against the Third Reich. A unique war in world
history. Never such a war took place. They want to die
fighting. We can't deny them this kind of death. By the way,
I didn't know at the time, a Jewish military organization
emerged. They didn't tell me about it, only that something is
going to happen. The Jews will fight. They need arms. We
approached the commander of the Home Army, the underground movement in Poland. Those arms were denied the
Jews. They can't be denied arms if such arms exist, and we
know you have arms. This message for the commander in

chief, General Sikorski, to issue orders that those arms will be given to the Jews.

This was another part of the mission. There are international Jewish leaders. Reach as many as possible, tell them this. They are Jewish leaders. Their people are dying. There will be no Jews, so what for do we need leaders? We are going to die as well. We don't try to escape. We stay here. Let them go to important offices—in London, wherever they are. Let them demand for action. If they refuse, let them walk out, stay in the street, refuse food, refuse drink. Let them die in view of all humanity. Who knows? Perhaps it will shake the conscience of the world.

Between those two Jewish leaders—somehow this belongs to human relations—I took, so to say, to the Bund leader, probably because of his behavior—he looked like a Polish no-bleman, a gentleman, with straight, beautiful gestures, dig-nified. I believe that he liked me also, personally. Now at a certain point, he said: "Mr. Vitold, I know the Western world. You are going to deal with the English. Now you will give them your oral reports. I am sure it will strengthen your report if you will be able to say 'I saw it myself.' We can organize for you to visit the Jewish ghetto. Would you do it? If you do, I will go with you to the Jewish ghetto in Warsaw so I will be sure you will be as safe as possible."

A few days later we established contact. By that time the Jewish ghetto as it existed in 1942 until July did not exist anymore. Out of approximately four hundred thousand Jews, some three hundred thousand were already deported from the ghetto. So within the outside walls, practically there were some four units. The most important was the so-called central ghetto. They were separated by some areas inhabited by the Aryans and already some areas not inhabited by anybody. There was a building. This building was constructed in such a way that the wall which separated the ghetto from the outside world was a part of the back of the building, so the front was facing the Aryan area. There was a tunnel. We went through this tunnel without any kind of difficulty. What struck me was that now he was a completely different man—the Bund leader, the Polish nobleman. I go with him. He is broken down, like a Jew from the ghetto, as if he had lived there all the time. Apparently, this was his nature. This was his world. So we walked the streets. He was on my left. We didn't talk very much. He led me. Well, so what? So now comes the description of it, yes? Well . . . naked bodies on the street. I ask him: "Why are they here?"

The corpses, you mean?

Corpses. He says: "Well, they have a problem. If a Jew dies and the family wants a burial, they have to pay tax on it. So they just throw them in the street."

Because they cannot pay the tax?

Yes. They cannot afford it. So then he says: "Every rag counts. So they take their clothing. And then once the body, the corpse, is on the street, the Judenrat has to take care of it."
    Women with their babies, publicly feeding their babies, but they have no . . . no breast, just flat. Babies with crazed eyes, looking . . .

Did it look like a completely strange world? Another world, I mean?

It was not a world. There was not humanity. Streets full, full. Apparently all of them lived in the street, exchanging what was the most important, everybody offering something to sell— three onions, two onions, some cookies. Selling. Begging each other. Crying and hungry. Those horrible children—some children running by themselves or with their mothers sitting. It wasn't humanity. It was some . . . some hell. Now in this part of the ghetto, the central ghetto, there were German officers. If the Gestapo released somebody, the Gestapo officers had to pass through the ghetto to get out of it. There were also Germans, German traffic. Now the Germans in uniform, they were walking . . . silence! Everybody frozen until he passed. No movement, no begging, nothing. Germans . . . contempt. This is apparent that they are subhuman. They are not human.

Now at a certain point some movement starts. Jews are running from the street I was on. We jumped into a house. He just hits the door. "Open the door! Open the door!" They open the door. We move in. Windows give onto the back of the street. We go to the opposite—in the door. Some woman opens the door. He says: "All right, all right, don't be afraid, we are Jews." He pushes me to the window, says "Look at it, look at it." There were two boys, nice looking boys, Hitlerjugend in uniform. They walked. Every step they made, Jews disappearing, running away. They were talking to each other. At a certain point a boy goes into his pocket without even thinking. Shoots! Some broken glass. The other boy congratulating him. They go back. So I was paralyzed. So then the Jewish woman—probably she recognized me, I don't know, that I am not a Jew—she embraced me. "Go, go, it doesn't do you any good, go, go." So we left the house. Then we left the ghetto. So then he said: "You didn't see everything; you didn't see too much. Would you like to go again? I will come with you. I want you to see everything. I will."

Next day we went again. The same house, the same way. So then again I was more conditioned, so I felt other things. Stench, stench, dirt, stench—everywhere, suffocating. Dirty streets, nervousness, tension. Bedlam. This was Platz Muranowski. In a corner of it some children were playing something with some rags—throwing the rags to one another. He says: "They are playing, you see. Life goes on. Life goes on." So then I said: "They are simulating playing. They don't play."

It was a special place for playing?

In the corner of Platz Muranowski—no, no, no, open. So I say: "They are . . ."

There are trees?

There were a few trees, rickety. So then we just walked the streets; we didn't talk to anybody. We walked probably one hour. Sometimes he would tell me: "Look at this Jew"—a Jew standing, without moving. I said: "Is he dead?" He says: "No, no, no, he is alive. Mr. Vitold, remember—he's dying, he's dying. Look at him. Tell them over there. You saw it. Don't forget." We walk again. It's macabre. Only from time to time he would whisper: "Remember this, remember this." Or he would tell me: "Look at her." Very many cases. I would say: "What are they doing here?" His answer: "They are dying, that's all. They are dying." And always: "But remember, remember."

We spent more time, perhaps one hour. We left the ghetto. Frankly, I couldn't take it anymore. "Get me out of it." And then I never saw him again. I was sick. Even now I don't want . . . I understand your role. I am here. I don't go back in my memory. I couldn't tell any more.

But I reported what I saw. It was not a world. It was not a part of humanity. I was not part of it. I did not belong there. I never saw such things, I never . . . nobody wrote about this kind of reality. I never saw any theater, I never saw any movie . . . this was not the world. I was told that these were human beings—they didn't look like human beings. Then we left. He embraced me then. "Good luck, good luck." I never saw him again.

Dr. Franz Grassler (Germany), deputy to Dr. Auerswald, Nazi commissioner of the Warsaw ghetto

You don't remember those days?

Not much. I recall more clearly my prewar mountaineering trips than the entire war period and those days in Warsaw. All in all, those were bad times. It's a fact: we tend to forget, thank God, the bad times more easily than the good. The bad times are repressed.

I'll help you remember. In Warsaw you were Dr. Auerswald's deputy.

Yes.

Dr. Auerswald was . . .

. . . commissioner of the "Jewish district" of Warsaw.

Dr. Grassler, this is Czerniakow's diary.* You're mentioned in it.

---

*Adam Czerniakow was president of the Judenrat (Jewish Council) of Warsaw.

It's been printed, it exists?

He kept a diary that was recently published. He wrote on July 7, 1941 . . .

July 7, 1941? That's the first time I've relearned a date. May I take notes? After all, it interests me too. So in July I was already there!

He wrote on July 7, 1941: ". . . morning at the Community, " that is, at the Jewish Council headquarters, ". . . and later with Auerswald, Schlosser . . ."

Schlosser was . . .

". . . and Grassler, on routine matters. " That's the first time . . .

. . . that my name is mentioned? Yes, but there were three of us. Schlosser was in . . . the "economic department." I think he had to do with economics.

And the second time was on July 22.

He wrote every day?

Yes, every day. It's quite amazing . . . .

That the diary was saved. It's amazing that it was saved.

Raul Hilberg

Adam Czerniakow began keeping a diary the very first week of the war, before the Germans entered Warsaw, and before he took over the responsibility of leading the Jewish community, and he kept his diary in daily entries until the afternoon of the day that he ended his life. He left us a window through which we can observe a Jewish community, the terminal hours of its life, a dying community, which began dying, from the beginning. And in that sense Adam Czerniakow did something very important. He didn't save the Jews—in that respect he was like other Jewish leaders—but he left us a record of what had happened to them in a day-by-day fashion. And you could see that he did all this on top of working a seven-day week, for he was a man without vacations, without any day off. And yet every day, almost every day, he had an entry. He might record the weather, where he went in the morning, and then all the things that happened. But he never failed to write. That was something that moved him, pushed him, compelled him throughout the years—almost three years—of his life under the Germans, and in that sense perhaps because he wrote in such a prosaic style we now know what went on in his mind, how things were perceived, recognized, reacted to.

We even know from what he didn't say just what it is that went through this community. There are constant references in the diary to the end. He talks in terms of Greek mythology, and he refers to himself as wearing a poisoned cloak, as Hercules once did. He has a feeling of doom for the Jews of Warsaw, and there are remarkable passages in the diary that illustrate what he meant. He is sarcastic enough, if that is the word, to remark in December of 1941 that now the intelligentsia were dying also. Up to this point poor people were dying, but by December 1941 members of the intelligentsia were starving to death. And he even has . . .

Why does he mention specifically the intelligentsia?

He mentions it because there is a difference, owing to the class structure within the ghetto, in vulnerability to starvation. The lower classes died first. The middle class died a little bit later. The intelligentsia were of course at the top of the middle class, and once they started dying the situation was really very, very bad. And that's the meaning of that. Now we're dealing with a ghetto where the average consumption was about 1200 calories, you see.

He mentions with approval, with approval, that one petitioner came to him for money and said: "I want money not in order to eat, I want money for the rent, to pay the rent for my apartment. I don't want to die in the street." This is the kind of comment that Czerniakow writes down in his diary: the meaning of dignity, the approval.

You mean he spoke of a petition from somebody? He said: "Give me money"?

Yes, but not for food. "Give me money so that I can pay the rent, because I don't want to die in the street." There were people dropping dead in the street. They were covered with newspaper.

Why was housing more important to him than food?

This particular individual wasn't eating enough to remain alive, and didn't want to be dying of hunger while collapsing in the street.

This means that death was not avoidable, as was dying outside?

Of course, of course, of course. It is one of these sardonic jokes of which he had quite a few. He always had strange description: of a band playing in front of a funeral parlor, of a hearse with drunken drivers, of a dead child running around the grounds. He had rather sardonic comments about death. He lived with death.

Dr. Franz Grassler

Did you go into the ghetto?

Seldom. When I had to visit Czerniakow.

What were the conditions like?

Awful. Yes, appalling. I never went back when I saw what it was like. Unless I had to. In the whole period I think I only went once or twice. We at the Commission tried to maintain the ghetto for its labor force, and especially to prevent epidemics, like typhus. That was the big danger.

Yes. Can you tell us about typhus?

I'm not a doctor. I only know that typhus is a very dangerous epidemic that wipes people out like the plague, and that it can't be confined to a ghetto. If typhus had broken out—I don't think it did, but there was fear that it might—it would have hit the Poles and the Germans.

Why was there typhus in the ghetto?

I don't know if there was, but there was a danger, because of the famine. People didn't get enough to eat. That's what was so awful. We at the Commission did our best to feed the ghetto, so it wouldn't become an incubator of epidemics. Aside from humanitarian factors, that's what mattered. If typhus had broken out—and it didn't—it wouldn't have stopped at the ghetto.

Czerniakow also wrote that one of the reasons the ghetto was walled in was because of this German fear.

Yes, absolutely! Fear of typhus.

He says Germans always associated Jews with typhus.

Maybe. I'm not sure if there were grounds for it. But imagine that mass of people packed in the ghetto. There weren't only the Warsaw Jews, but others who came later. The danger kept on growing.

Raul Hilberg

There was a lady somewhere in Warsaw in love with a man, and the man was hit, grievously wounded, with his insides coming out. This woman stuffed the insides back with her own hands. She carried the man to a first-aid station. He died. He was buried in a mass grave. She disinterred him and buried him. This, to Czerniakow—this simple episode—was the ultimate of virtue.

He is never revolted?

He doesn't bother. Or he doesn't express the revolt; he doesn't express the disgust except with other Jews, Jews who either deserted the community by emigrating early, or Jews who like Ganzweich collaborated with the Germans. And for the Germans he doesn't have words of disgust. I think he's beyond such words. He hasn't any criticism of the Germans themselves, and only seldom allows himself to make a remark which indicates that he opposed something by arguing. He very seldom argues with the Germans. He pleads, he appeals, but he doesn't argue with them. He does argue when he's forced not only to build the wall but to pay for it. And he says that if the wall is being put up as a hygienic measure to prevent Jewish epidemics from engulfing the Polish or German population outside, then why is it, why is it that the Jews have to pay for it? The people who get the protection should be paying for the medicine. If the wall is medicine, let the Germans pay. And Auerswald, the ghetto commissar, says that's a very nice argument that he, Czerniakow, might bring up at an international conference some day, but for now he'll pay for the wall. Czerniakow writes all this down, including Auerswald's reply to his own argument. And that's about the most he ever allows himself to say in criticism of what the Germans are doing. So he takes for granted, he assumes, he anticipates everything that is happening to the Jews, including the worst.

Dr. Franz Grassler

The Germans had a policy on the Warsaw ghetto. What was that policy?

You're asking more than I know. The policy that wound up
with extermination, the "final solution"—we knew nothing
about it, of course. Our job was to maintain the ghetto and try
to preserve the Jews as a work force. The Commissariat's goal
in fact, was very different from the one that later led to extermination.

*Yes, but do you know how many people died in the ghetto each
month in 1941?*

I don't know now, if I ever knew.

But you did know. There are exact figures.

I probably knew . . .

Yes. Five thousand a month.

Five thousand a month? Yes, well . . .

That's a lot.

That's a lot, of course. But there were far too many people in
the ghetto. That was it.

Far too many.

Far too many.

*My question is philosophical. What does a ghetto mean, in your
opinion?*

History is full of ghettos, going back centuries, for all I know.
Persecution of the Jews wasn't a German invention, and it

didn't start with World War II. The Poles persecuted them too.

But a ghetto like Warsaw's, in a great capital, in the heart of the city . . .

That was unusual.

You say you wanted to maintain the ghetto.

Our mission wasn't to annihilate the ghetto, but to keep it alive, to maintain it.

What does "alive" mean in such conditions?

That was the problem. That was the whole problem.

But people were dying in the streets. There were bodies everywhere.

Exactly. That was the paradox.

You see it as a paradox?

I'm sure of it.

Why? Can you explain?

No.

Why not?

Explain what? But the fact is . . .

That wasn't "maintaining"! Jews were being exterminated daily in the ghetto. Czerniakow wrote . . .

To maintain it properly we'd have needed more substantial rations and less crowding.

Why weren't the rations more humane? Why weren't they? That was a German decision, wasn't it?

There was no real decision to starve the ghetto. The big decision to exterminate came much later.

That's right, later. In 1942.

Precisely!

A year later.

Just so. Our mission, as I recall it, was to manage the ghetto, and naturally with those inadequate rations and the overcrowding, a high, even excessive death rate was inevitable.

Yes. What does "maintain" the ghetto mean in such conditions: the food, sanitation, etcetera? What could the Jews do against such measures?

They couldn't do anything.

Raul Hilberg

Czerniakow saw a film before the war where the captain of a sinking ship gives an order to the orchestra to play jazz. In the entry of July 8, 1942, not even two weeks before his death, he identifies himself with this captain of the sinking ship.

Yes, yes . . .

Of course there is no jazz but there is a kind of children's festival . . .

Chess tournaments, yes. There's theater, a children's festival, there's everything going on until the last moment. But more importantly, these are symbols. These outward cultural activities, these festivals, they're not simply morale-building devices, which is what Czerniakow identifies them to be. Rather, they are symbolic of the entire posture of the ghetto, which is in the process of healing or trying to heal sick people who are soon going to be gassed, which is trying to educate youngsters who will never be growing up, which is in the process of trying to find work for people and increase employment in a situation which is doomed to failure. They are going on as though life were continuing. They have an official faith in the survivability of the ghetto, even after all indications are to the contrary. The strategy continues to be: "We must continue, for this is the only strategy that is left. We must minimize the injury, minimize the damage, minimize the losses, but we must continue." And continuity is the only thing in all of this.

But obviously when he compares himself to this captain of a sinking ship, he knows that everything . . .

He knows, he knows. I think he knew or he sensed or he believed the end was coming, perhaps as early as October 1941, when he has a note about alarming rumors as to the fate of Warsaw Jewry in the spring. This is also when Bischoff, the head of the transfer office, tells him that, after all, the ghetto is only a temporary device, without specifying for what. He knows because in January he has premonitions or reports or rumors about Lithuanians coming. He is concerned when Auerswald disappears and is going to Berlin, right around January 20, 1942, which we now know to have been the date of the "final solution" conference in Berlin, the Wannsee Conference. And even though Czerniakow in Warsaw, behind the walls, has no idea of such a conference going on in Berlin, yet he is concerned that Auerswald, the ghetto commissar, is going to Berlin. He can't imagine why, unless it is for a purpose that bodes no good. And so in February there are more rumors. In March the rumors are becoming even more specific. He now begins to record the departure of Jews from the Lublin ghetto, or Mielec, or Krakow, and Lvov. And he recognizes that something may well be in the offing for Warsaw itself. And every subsequent entry is replete with the anxiety that he feels.

When Czerniakow hears rumors about the deportations from Lublin, Lvov, and Krakow around March 1942—and we now know that the transports went to Belzec—does he ask in his diary where they are shipped, what happens to them?

He never does. He never mentions any destination. But we cannot really decide that he had no knowledge whatsoever about these camps. All we know is that he didn't mention them in the diary. And we also know, of course, from other sources that the existence of death camps was already known in Warsaw, certainly by June.

Dr. Franz Grassler

Why did Czerniakow commit suicide?

Because he realized there was no future for the ghetto. He probably saw before I did that the Jews would be killed. I suppose the Jews already had their excellent secret services. They were too well informed, better than we were.

Think so?

Yes, I do.

The Jews knew more than you?

I'm convinced of it!

It's hard to believe.

The German administration was never informed of what would happen to the Jews.

When was the first deportation to Treblinka?

Before Auerswald's suicide, I think.

Auerswald's?

I mean Czerniakow's. Sorry.

July 22.

Those are dates . . . So the deportations began July 22, 1942.

Yes.

To Treblinka.

And Czerniakow killed himself July 23.

Yes, that is the next day. So that was it: he'd realized that his idea—it was his idea, I think—of working in good faith with the Germans, in the Jews' best interests—he'd realized this idea, this dream, was destroyed.

That the idea was a dream.

Yes. And when the dream faded, he took the logical way out.

Raul Hilberg

The last entry takes place how long before his suicide?

The last entry precedes his death by a few hours.

What does he write?

"It is three o'clock. So far four thousand are ready to go. The orders are that there must be nine thousand by four o'clock." This is the last entry of a man on the afternoon of the day that he commits suicide.

The first transport of the Jews of Warsaw for Treblinka was the twenty-second of July, 1942, and he committed suicide the day after.

That's right. In other words, on the twenty-second, you see, on the twenty-second he is called in by Sturmbahnführer Höfle, who is in charge of the resettlement staff, who has come in there for the express purpose of taking the Jews out of Warsaw. Höfle tells him, on the twenty-second, . . . And here, incidentally, is another fascinating point: Czerniakow is so agitated that he doesn't put the dates down correctly—instead of saying July 22, 1942, he says July 22, 1940. Höfle calls him in at ten o'clock, disconnects the telephones, children are removed from the playground opposite the community building, and then he is told that all Jews irrespective of sex and age, with certain exceptions, will be deported to the east. To the east. Again the east. And that by 4 P.M. today a contingent of six thousand people must be provided. And this at the minimum will be the daily quota. Now he is told that at ten in the morning of July 22, 1942. He then goes on. He keeps appealing. He wants certain exemptions. He wants the council staff to be exempt. He wants the staff of the welfare organizations to be exempt, and he is terribly worried that the orphans will be deported, and repeatedly brings up the orphans. And on the next day he still doesn't have assurance that the orphans are going to be saved. Now if he cannot be the caretaker of the orphans, then he has lost his war, he has lost his struggle.

Why the orphans?

They are the most helpless element in the community. They are the little children, its future, who have lost their parents. They cannot possibly do anything on their own. If the orphans do not have exemption, if he doesn't even get the promise, the words spoken by a German SS officer, not even assurances which as he knows cannot be counted, if he cannot even get the words, what can he think?

If he cannot take care of the children, what else can he do?

Some people report that he wrote a note after he closed the book on the diary in which he said: "They want me to kill the children with my own hands."

Dr. Franz Grassler

Did you think this idea of a ghetto was a good one? A sort of self-management?

That's right.

A mini-state?

It worked well.

But it was self-management for death, wasn't it?

We know that now. But at the time . . .

Even then!

No!

Czerniakow wrote: "We're puppets, we have no power."

Yes.

"No power."

Sure . . . that was . . .

You Germans were the overlords.

Yes.

The overlords. The masters.

Obviously.

Czerniakow was merely a tool.

Yes, but a good tool. Jewish self-management worked well, I
can tell you.

*It worked well for three years: 1941, 1942, 1943 . . . two and a
half years. And in the end . . .*

In the end . . .

"Worked well" for what? To what end?

For self-preservation.

No! For death!

Yes, but . . .

Self-management, self-preservation . . . for death!

That's easy to say now.

*You admitted the conditions were inhuman. Atrocious . . . horri-
ble!*

Yes.

So it was clear even then . . .

No! Extermination wasn't clear. Now we see the result.

Extermination isn't so simple. One step was taken, then another, and another, and another . . .

Yes.

But to understand the process, one must . . .

I repeat: extermination did not take place in the ghetto, not at first. Only with the evacuations.

Evacuations?

The evacuations to Treblinka. The ghetto could have been wiped out with weapons, as was finally done after the rebellion. After I'd left. But at the start . . . Mr. Lanzmann, this is getting us nowhere. We're reaching no new conclusions.

I don't think we can.

I didn't know then what I know now.

You weren't a nonentity.

But I was!

You were important.

You overestimate my role.

No. You were second to the commissioner of the Warsaw "Jewish district."

But I had no power.

It was something.

You were part of the vast German power structure.

Correct. But a small part. You overestimate the authority of a deputy of twenty-eight then.

You were thirty.

Twenty-eight.

At thirty you were mature.

Yes, but for a lawyer who got his degree at twenty-seven, it's just a beginning.

You had a doctorate.

The title proves nothing.

Did Auerswald have one too?

No. But the title's irrelevant.

Doctor of Law . . . What did you do after the war?

I was with a mountaineering publishing house. I wrote and published mountain guide books. I published a mountain climbers' magazine.

Is climbing your main interest?

Yes.

The mountains, the air . . .

Yes.

The sun, the pure air . . .

Not like the ghetto air.

**Gertrude Schneider and her mother (New York),
survivors of the ghetto**

> "The words I write you
>   Are written with tears, not ink.

Years, the best years, are finished
And gone—never to be recovered.
It's difficult to repair what has been destroyed.
It's difficult to tie up the bonds of our love.
Ah, look, your tears,
The fault is not mine.
Because that's how it must be.
That's how it must be, that's how it must be.
We must part from one another.
That's how it must be, that's how it must be.
Love must end for both of us.
Do you remember when I
Left you on the road?
My fate told me I had to leave you,
Because I never want to stand in that road again.
Because that's how it must be."

Lohame Haghettaot Kibbutz Museum (Ghetto Fighters' Kibbutz), Israel

The Jewish Combat Organization (JCO) in the Warsaw ghetto was officially formed on July 28, 1942. After the first mass deportation to Treblinka, which was interrupted on September 30, some sixty thousand Jews remained in the ghetto. On January 18, 1943, the deportations were resumed. Despite a severe lack of weapons, the members of the JCO called for resistance, and started fighting, to the Germans' total surprise. It lasted three days. The Nazis withdrew with losses, abandoning weapons the Jews grabbed. The deportations were stopped. The Germans now knew they had to fight to conquer the ghetto. The battle began on the evening of April 19, 1943, the eve of Pessach (Passover). It had to be a fight to the death.

Itzhak Zuckermann (known as "Antek"), second-in-command of the JCO, at the Lohame Haghettaot Kibbutz Museum (Ghetto Fighters' Kibbutz), Israel

I began drinking after the war. It was very difficult. Claude, you asked for my impression. If you could lick my heart, it would poison you.

At the request of Mordechaï Anielewicz, commander-in-chief of the JCO, Antek had left the ghetto six days before the German attack. His mission: to ask Polish Resistance leaders to arm the Jews. They refused.

In fact, I left the ghetto six days before the uprising. I wanted to return on the nineteenth, the eve of Passover. I wrote to Mordechaï Anielewicz and to Zivia. Zivia was my wife. I got back a very polite letter, very formal, from Anielewicz, and a very aggressive letter from Zivia that said: "You haven't done a thing so far. Nothing." I decided to go back anyway. I had no idea what was going on in the ghetto. I couldn't imagine it. But Simha's companions knew of the German encirclement before I did.

Simha Rottem (known as "Kajik")

At Passover time we felt something was going to happen in the ghetto. We could feel the pressure. On Passover eve the Germans attacked. Not just the Germans, but the Ukrainians too, along with the Lithuanians, the Polish police, and the Latvians, and this massive force entered the ghetto. We felt this was the end. On the morning the Germans went into the ghetto, the attack was concentrated on the central ghetto. We were a little away from it; we heard blasts, shots, the echo of the gunfire, and we knew the fighting was fierce in the central ghetto.

During the first three days of fighting, the Jews had the upper hand. The Germans retreated at once to the ghetto entrance, carrying dozens of wounded with them. From then on, their onslaught came entirely from the outside, through air attack and artillery. We couldn't resist the bombing, especially their method of setting fire to the ghetto. The whole ghetto was ablaze. All life vanished from the streets and houses. We hid in the cellars and bunkers. From there we made our sorties. We went out at night. The Germans were in the ghetto mostly by day, leaving at night. They were afraid to enter the ghetto at night.

The bunkers were prepared by the residents, not by the fighters. When we could no longer stay in the streets, we fell back on the bunkers. All the bunkers were alike inside. The most striking thing was the crowding, for there were a lot of us, and the heat. It was so hot you couldn't breathe. Not even a candle could burn in those bunkers. To breathe in that intense heat, you sometimes had to lie with your face to the ground. The fact that we fighters hadn't prepared bunkers proves we didn't expect to survive our fight against the Germans.

I don't think the human tongue can describe the horror we went through in the ghetto. In the streets, if you can call them that, for nothing was left of the streets, we had to step over heaps of corpses. There was no room to get around them. Besides fighting the Germans, we fought hunger, and thirst. We had no contact with the outside world; we were completely isolated, cut off from the world. We were in such a state that we could no longer understand the very meaning of why we went on fighting. We thought of attempting a breakout to the Aryan part of Warsaw, outside the ghetto.

Just before May 1 Sigmund and I were sent to try to contact Antek in Aryan Warsaw. We found a tunnel under Bonifratérska Street that led out into Aryan Warsaw. Early in the morning we suddenly emerged into a street in broad daylight. Imagine us on that sunny May 1, stunned to find ourselves in the street, among normal people. We'd come from another planet. People immediately jumped on us, because we certainly looked exhausted, skinny, in rags. Around the ghetto there were always suspicious Poles who grabbed Jews. By a miracle, we escaped them. In Aryan Warsaw, life went on as naturally and normally as before. The cafés operated normally, the restaurants, buses, streetcars, and movies were open. The ghetto was an isolated island amid normal life.

Our job was to contact Itzhak Zuckermann to try to mount a rescue operation, to try to save the few fighters who might still be alive in the ghetto. We managed to contact Zuckermann. We found two sewer workers. On the night of May 8–9 we decided to return to the ghetto with another buddy, Rijek, and the two sewer men. After the curfew we entered the sewers. We were entirely at the mercy of the two workmen, since only they knew the ghetto's underground layout. Halfway there they decided to turn back, they tried to drop us, and we had to threaten them with our guns. We went on through the sewers until one of the workmen told us we were under the ghetto. Rijek guarded them so they couldn't escape. I raised the manhole cover to go up into the ghetto.

At bunker Mila 18,* I missed them by a day. I had returned the night of May 8–9. The Germans found the bunker on the morning of the eighth. Most of its survivors committed suicide, or succumbed to gas in the bunkers. I went to bunker Franczis-kanska 22. There was no answer when I yelled the password, so I had to go on through the ghetto. I suddenly heard a woman calling from the ruins. It was darkest night, no lights, you saw nothing. All the houses were in ruins, and I heard only one voice. I thought some evil spell had been cast on me, a woman's voice talking from the rubble. I circled the ruins. I didn't look at my watch, but I must have spent a half hour exploring, trying to find the woman whose voice guided me, but unfortunately I didn't find her.

Were there fires?

Strictly speaking, no, for the flames had died down, but there was still smoke, and that awful smell of charred flesh of people who had surely been burned alive. I continued on my way, going to other bunkers in search of fighting units, but it was the same everywhere. I'd give the password: "Jan."

That's a Polish first name, Jan?

Right. And I got no answer. I went from bunker to bunker, and after walking for hours in the ghetto, I went back toward the sewers.

Was he alone then?

---

*The bunker Mila 18 was the headquarters of the Jewish Combat Organization.

Yes, I was alone all the time. Except for that woman's voice, and a man I met as I came out of the sewers, I was alone throughout my tour of the ghetto. I didn't meet a living soul. At one point I recall feeling a kind of peace, of serenity. I said to myself: "I'm the last Jew. I'll wait for morning, and for the Germans."